RECOLLECTIONS OF OTHER DAYS

Memories of Robert Adams, William Adams,
Andrew Anderson, Anna Moore Schwien, Eli Merriman,
E. H Caldwell, W. S. Rankin, Annie Marie Kelly,
Thomas Noakes, Mrs. Delmas Givens, Ruth Dodson,
J. Frank Dobie, Roy Terrell, Louis Rawalt

i

RECOLLECTIONS

Memories of Robert Adams, William Adams,
Andrew Anderson, Anna Moore Schwien,
Eli Merriman, E. H Caldwell, W. S. Rankin,
Annie Marie Kelly, Thomas Noakes,
Mrs. Delmas Givens, Ruth Dodson,
J. Frank Dobie, Roy Terrell, Louis Rawalt

OF OTHER DAYS

Edited by
Murphy Givens & Jim Moloney

NUECES PRESS
Corpus Christi, Texas

Library of Congress Control Number 2013943749

Givens, Murphy and Jim Moloney

RECOLLECTIONS OF OTHER DAYS: Memories of Robert Adams, William Adams, Andrew Anderson, Anna Moore Schwien, Eli Merriman, E. H Caldwell, W. S. Rankin, Annie Marie Kelly, Thomas Noakes, Mrs. Delmas Givens, Ruth Dodson, J. Frank Dobie, Roy Terrell, Louis Rawalt.

Includes index.

   1. South Texas — History.   2. Nueces County — History.
   2. Corpus Christi — History.

ISBN   978-0-9832565-4-0

Published by Nueces Press, Corpus Christi, Texas.

Cover design by Jeff Chilcoat

Page ii: In 1897, people gathered on Mesquite Street in front of the Bidwell Hotel to throw snowballs during a rare snowfall in Corpus Christi.

www.nuecespress.com

We dedicate this book to the memory of Marie Blucher who interviewed and compiled many of the memoirs and had the foresight to place copies in the Corpus Christi Public Library for use by future generations of historians.

I went through a lot of hardships the early part of my life. I guess that is why I'm still here.... I went to sleep many nights not knowing whether I would be alive next morning or not.

— Robert Adams

We didn't use to think anything of saddling up a horse and getting a wallet, cup and blanket, and wherever night came you would unsaddle and sleep. I have slept out many a night, using my saddle for a pillow.

— William Adams

I used to be good at gigging fish. One day one of the Indian soldiers borrowed my gig and began throwing it towards my foot, each time striking the ground just an inch or two from my toe. He certainly had me dancing around.

— Andrew Anderson

While the house was burning I had to stand and watch from my retreat by the fence the huge tongues of flames shoot heavenward, knowing they were licking up the fruits of ten years toil and everything, except ourselves, that I valued in the world.

— Thomas Noakes

"If you have any business that needs attention, you had better return to your home in Texas and take care of it." He leafed through a chart on his desk. "Prognosis: six months." The surgeon looked straight at me.

— Louis Rawalt

EDITORS' NOTE

It is perhaps only natural that those of us who study history sometimes get the urge to rescue fugitive pieces, long languishing in the files, and confine them in one neat, easily accessible place, like between the covers of a book.

Many of the pieces included in this volume are well-known to local historians. They have been looked at and quoted over the years, in stray bits and pieces, but they have never been printed, not in their entirety. Some of the recollections were compiled by Marie von Blucher of Corpus Christi's La Retama Library after interviewing the subjects between 1939 and 1941. Other biographical pieces were collected to round out the volume.

We have not changed the words used or amended the style in which they were voiced. However, the narrators, especially those who were interviewed, were speaking from memory of events long ago. At times, they got their dates wrong or facts confused. We have tried to set the record straight through footnotes. They may seem pedantic, but there was no easy or simple way for the editors to interpose themselves in the manuscript without seeming to be a "know-it-all." We do have the luxury of being able to check the facts against various sources and the historical record. If there are mistakes in the main text, you can ascribe them to the narrators and authors. If there are mistakes in the footnotes, you can lay the responsibility on the editors.

This is a collection of recollections or memories of old times and early days in Corpus Christi and at least one area of the Nueces Valley. It's too bad that a good title for this book was already taken by the French novelist Marcel Proust in "Remembrance of Things Past" or another one by the Russian writer Vladimir Nabokov in his autobiography "Speak, Memory." The two titles suggest the essence of this book.

Murphy Givens

Jim Moloney

CONTENTS

CHAPTER 1

ROBERT ADAMS
HARD LICKS

I was born on March 9, 1847 in Norfolk, England, and have been in this country going on 87 years. My father, Robert Adams, my mother, my brothers, William and Harry, my sister Elizabeth, and I came over in 1852. Why did my father and mother come over here? What made them leave England? Why, Colonel Kinney's pamphlets![1] (Plate 2) I'm glad we came. It was overpopulated over there.

We crossed the Atlantic in an old square-rigged sailing vessel, and it took between seven or eight weeks to make the voyage. I wasn't scared — I was too small. But I do remember that it was pretty rough and we would go from side to side in our bunks. We were cabin passengers; there were 400 Germans in the hold. There was one death on the boat, coming over, and they buried the person at sea. We landed at New Orleans in November, from where we went on to Galveston on an old side-wheeler. We came to Corpus Christi on a mail boat, which was just a small one-mast ship.

---

[1] Corpus Christi founder Henry Kinney distributed handbills in England and Scotland offering land for sale. Kinney's package deal was 100 acres of land at one dollar an acre. With the 100 acres, the buyer would get one yoke of oxen, one horse, 10 cows, and one town lot in Nuecestown, 12 miles upriver from Corpus Christi.

We stayed in Corpus Christi only about a week, and then went to the country, where we lived for several years at three different locations, my father being engaged in farming. Our last place in the country was near Judge Webb's place, several miles from Corpus, now called Avery Point.[2] After a year or two we moved to town, where my father built a home just a little west of the courthouse.

When I came to Corpus there were three little stores there. Old lady Hart[3] had one on the beach close to where the Nueces Hotel is now, old man Noessel[4] had a small store on Chaparral Street, and Norris had a store on the hill. There were just a few scattered houses along the streets. Toward the south, right out from the Meuly house, there used to be a plaza, something like Artesian Square, used for entertainments, I think. The town was called Kinney's Ranch, and I think it wasn't over 125 or 135 in population. Chaparral Street was not called by its name then, but it was soon after.

There was a meat pickling plant away up on North Beach, then called the Rincon. It had vats and everything needed to take care of hides, and boilers in which the meat was put to be cured. The concrete vats in which the hides were salted were rectangular in shape and divided by partitions. The plant was already out of use when I came, but was afterwards used for a slaughter house. Only one beef a day was killed here, as that was enough to feed everybody. A plant for preserving meat was operated by the Hopsons[5] about where the Nueces Hotel is now. They cured and smoked it in a house made especially for that purpose. They also pickled it. They shipped their products out. When we first came,

---

[2] James Webb served as Secretary of Treasury, Secretary of State, and Attorney General of the Republic of Texas. He moved to Corpus Christi after his daughter Mary Elizabeth married Henry Kinney and he was appointed Judge of the 14th Judicial District. Webb County (Laredo) was named for him.

[3] Elizabeth Hart opened her store in 1848 in Gen. Taylor's old commissary building. She later built a concrete store and dwelling above it on Water Street.

[4] George Noessel came to Corpus Christi in 1848 and bought the Kinney House, a hotel built by Henry Kinney in 1845, and turned it into a grocery store in 1855.

[5] C.R. Hopson's meat-packing plant was at the corner of Peoples and Water. Henry Kinney was a partner in the enterprise.

the government had headquarters[6] in Corpus Christi. They used to take supplies by regular mule trains all the way to Fort Merrill, on the Nueces River in Live Oak County, and to Fort Ewell in La Salle County. The United States troops used to keep pickets out at the edge of town at night on account of the Indians. Mother would hear the coyotes howling and feared the Indians were coming. I never did see any Indians close by, although once I saw some going up a hill in single file, in later years.

When I came to Corpus Christi, the Gravises were already there. Mrs. Gravis[7] was a widow and kept a hotel, the only one in Corpus Christi; we called it a tavern. The Baldeschwilers[8] were there, too. Andrew Baldeschwiler died over in San Patricio several years ago. There was Peter, too. The old lady was probably a widow when I came to Corpus Christi. B. F. Neal[9] printed the paper, being one of the earliest newspapermen in Corpus Christi. I recall the Chapman house on the bluff, but don't remember Colonel Kinney's house. Colonel Fullerton lived in Corpus, too, long ago. The Ohlers[10] lived on the hill. One day I went up there, and they were making soap. I saw him making it; he was cooking it in a large cast iron pot. It was yellow, and was sold there in the town.

Belden and Gilpin[11] owned that old house, not far from the Meuly place, where the Eureka Laundry was later. When Cortina[12]

---

[6] Gen. Persifor Smith, commander of the Eighth Military District, moved his headquarters from San Antonio to Corpus Christi in 1853. Army supplies were shipped to Corpus Christi and freighted to U.S. forts on the Texas frontier.

[7] John A.F. Gravis, a Texas Ranger during the Revolution, moved to Corpus Christi and worked as a builder and bricklayer with Henry Berry. After he died in a yellow fever epidemic in 1854, his widow Irenah married his business partner Berry and operated the Berry boarding house.

[8] Blaize and Teresa Baldeschwiler arrived in Corpus Christi in 1845, when Zachary Taylor's army was camped outside the town. Mrs. Baldeschwiler claimed that her son Andrew, born on April 13, 1846, was the first Anglo child born in Corpus Christi. Mrs. Baldeschwiler was a cook employed by the army and Mr. Baldeschwiler was a carpenter and woodcarver.

[9] Benjamin F. Neal moved to Corpus Christi in 1844. In 1850 he established the newspaper *Nueces Valley* and in 1852 he was elected mayor.

[10] Edward Ohler, a merchant, moved to Corpus Christi in 1848 and opened a store at Peoples and Water and he built a wharf out into the bay from there.

[11] Frederick Belden and H.A. Gilpin.

was expected, they fortified that place of Belden and Gilpin's. Cortina didn't get to Corpus, but we were frightened, all right, as it was reported he was coming to take the city. I had a broken leg and couldn't get away. I guess that was about 1857 or 1858.

Old Peter Mireur was living in Corpus Christi in those days, Joe's father. I think he was a brick mason or something like that. The Kinghorns lived there for a while. He was a wheelwright. Jim Barnard, Frank's father, had a saloon on Chaparral Street in the early days.[13] The old concrete house built by Ranahan, a brick mason, I remember; FitzSimmons lived in it later on.[14]

I knew of D. S. Howard and Col. Moore,[15] who were interested in a canal down there in what they called the mudflats,[16] where they come out of Aransas Bay to Corpus Christi Bay. They had a dredge to dig the canal with. I went through there once with my father. They were mudflats sure enough. Everything behind the boat was just loblolly — thick mud.

The Noessels were in Corpus then. I remember two sons, Felix and Otto. Otto died of tuberculosis. And there were the Dixes; Capt. Dix had three sons — John, who married Miss Fannie McNeil, Oliver, and Theodore, and a daughter who married Mr. Russell. The first schoolteacher I knew in Corpus Christi was old man Craft.[17] He taught in a red-brick building on Water Street, near where the

---

[12] Juan Nepomoceno Cortina and followers caused considerable alarm in 1857 and 1858 with attacks throughout the lower Rio Grande. Rangers were sent to quell the violence.

[13] James R. Barnard, a Mexican War correspondent and early Corpus Christi newspaperman, owned the La Retama Saloon, where a fracas in 1860 ended with the shooting death of Deputy Tom Nolan. The saloon on Chaparral was across the street from the Sierra Madre Hotel.

[14] James Ranahan's shellcrete house was built in 1853 at the intersection of Mesquite and Taylor. It was torn down to make way for a parking lot for the Ritz Theater, which opened in 1929.

[15] Dean S. Howard, who came from New York, and Col. John M. Moore, who came from Alabama, were partners in an effort to dredge a ship channel across the bay, work that first began with Henry Kinney and his nephew Somers Kinney.

[16] The mudflats were later known as Turtle Cove.

[17] M. P. Craft was the principal of a school started by Charles Lovenskiold, which opened in the Ohler building on Water Street in 1853.

Nueces Hotel laundry is now (600 block). Everybody paid for tuition.

There was an old couple named Holthaus. He was German and she was French. They were bakers, having their shop a little north of the present site of the Nueces Hotel.

On the first July Fourth that I spent in America, we went across the bay in Capt. Dix's schooner to old Capt. Hatch's.[18] My! What good ice-rind watermelons he used to grow. We would thump them and they would pop right open. Coming back, the bay was so rough we had lots of water thrown over us.

When I was eight years old it was arranged that I would live in the home of Samuel Colon, for clothing and food. He was a freighter who shipped goods out of Corpus by ox-cart to all parts of the country. He was living in town then; later he moved to Nuecestown and I went with him. He gave me six months schooling while we were at Nuecestown. I guess that was my recompense for all the work I did. And that was all the schooling I ever had. I got my learning by hard licks, not by theory.

One time Colon broke my leg. He would have broken my neck if George Reynolds hadn't interfered. It happened on George Reynolds' porch at Nuecestown. There were five or six yoke of oxen hitched to the wagon and some of them weren't very gentle. Colon told me to unhitch them and I didn't go to do it. He picked me up and threw me down on the floor so hard it broke my leg. I crawled away under the porch. The oxen went off with the wagon and were gone all night, hitched to the wagon, but were found next morning.

Colon was drunk and angry when he treated me the way he did. They didn't set my leg, just bandaged it up. After a while I walked with one crutch and a cane, but it would break time and again. It would wobble at the broken place when I tried to walk, and sometimes the splintered bone in my flesh would hurt. It was six months healing.

---

[18] John James Dix, who came to Texas in 1837, built a house on Water Street. George C. Hatch was an early settler and farmer in the Ingleside area.

I went through a lot of hardships the early part of my life. I guess that is why I'm still here. People don't know what hard times are, nowadays. They think they do, but they don't. People were more generous and sociable in those days. I guess the hard times they went through together made them that way. They weren't envious as they are now. In those days there was no bank in Corpus. If you wanted to borrow, say, $500, you would go to a friend who had that much, and ask him to lend it to you, and he wouldn't hesitate at all, wouldn't even require a note. And when the time came to pay it back, you would pay it back. A man's word in those days was worth more than a note is now.

In the country around Corpus Christi were a number of farms and small ranches. Old man Priour[19] lived out there at Salt Lake, where he had a garden of seven or eight acres, from which he supplied the people of Corpus Christi with vegetables. His wife was the daughter of old lady Hart, who had a store in Corpus Christi.

Out where Avery Point is now, Judge Webb lived. They should have called it Webb Point, for he built quite a place out there. I knew Judge Webb's son Tom, for I lived with him for one year on his farm near Helena, which is on the road from Indianola to San Antonio. All the goods freighted from Indianola to San Antonio[20] passed right by his farm and I saw a great deal of it pass. I never lived at home again, as that year weaned me away.

The Britton[21] place was down on the Oso. It was called the Britton Motts. A man named Worthington married one of Mrs. Britton's daughters. The Pettigrews had a little ranch on the Oso — all that was open country then. Down at Peñascal,[22] which is now in Kenedy's Pasture, some merchants kept stocks of stores for the

---

[19] Jean Marie Priour, a Breton, married Rosalie Bridget Hart, daughter of Elizabeth Hart. The Priours' farm was at the Salt Lake, a mile west of town. It dried up during a prolonged drought during the Civil War.

[20] The Old Cart Road, also known as the Old Freight Road, the Goliad Road, and the Mexican Cart Trail, ran from Indianola to Victoria to Goliad to Helena to Floresville and San Antonio.

[21] Forbes Britton, merchant, state senator and Mexican War veteran.

[22] Peñascal was a small settlement 60 miles south of Corpus Christi on Baffin Bay.

ranches, but I don't remember their names now. The Tinneys — Bill, Tom and Sam — had a ranch near Piedras Pintas. Margaret Tinney married Fritz Werner and another Tinney girl married Chris Yung.

Other ranches in this section were started by some of the English families who came over about the time we did. James Bryden[23] came in 1851, I think. The Brydens lived for many years two miles above Santa Gertrudis Creek. He was in charge of Major Chapman's sheep. Joseph Almond and his wife and son Joseph came on our boat. Almond lived at the Barbon, a small dry creek that emptied into Casa Blanca. After I married, I lived there for a couple of years, while my brother and I took care of Almond's sheep when he moved to Corpus.[24] Joseph Almond married a Miss Wade. Mr. and Mrs. Wade also came from England about this time. They also lived at Casa Blanca. Their son John married Miss Beynon.

The country in this section was beautiful, with grass three to four feet high. It was a wild grass that made good hay. A number of people, among them old man Rankin[25] (W. S. Rankin's father) and old man Hoffman, a barber, sold this hay to persons who brought freight teams to town. They would mow the grass down with a scythe and bring it in on a horse cart. Chaparral Street used to be full of wagons in the early days, especially in the 1860s, 1870s and 1880s, and there was a good demand for this hay for the mules and horses.

When I was a boy, and living with Mr. Colon in Nuecestown, I used to help gather salt in the lagoons of Laguna Madre at Laureles or sometimes in the Oso. When water came in high, it filled all the shallow lakes, and when it receded the salt could be gathered.

---

[23] James Bryden, a sheepman from Scotland, was hired to handle Maj. William Chapman's sheep. He was given a share of the increase and in time owned his own flocks. He later worked for King Ranch.

[24] Joseph Almond returned to live in Corpus Christi in 1867 to do carpentry work. It was bad timing. He moved to town just as a yellow fever epidemic hit. He recorded the deaths each day in his diary.

[25] James T. Rankin operated a livery stable on Mesquite. He died of yellow fever in 1867.

The salt was in small grains, about the size of peas, and you had to rake it up out of the water, which was about two inches deep. We would pile the salt on the bank and let it drain, and then later put it into sacks or buckets and take it to the wagons. But it wasn't dry even then, and the salty water would ooze out of the bags of wet salt carried across my shoulders, so that most of the time I was dripping with saltwater. In addition to this coarse salt, there was a finer quality, like table salt, that was formed when the wind would blow up the small rivulets bordering the lagoons, leaving the salt on the shores.

The wagons used for hauling the salt were drawn by six yoke of oxen. We would go up the old salt road, which ran from the lakes by Laureles[26] and on to Nuecestown. Here it was stored away in a small house to be sold. Most of it was exchanged, though, not sold. All of north Texas had to come down to Corpus[27] to get salt, for home use and for their stock. These people would trade for it, as they had no money. In exchange for the salt, they would give bacon, meal, or any commodity they had.

Quite a bit of Mr. Colon's freight went to San Patricio and to Rancho Grande, which was on this side of the river opposite San Patricio. About a half mile this side of Rancho Grande, on the main traveled road, old lady Daugherty (or Dawtry, more probably the latter, as there was some connection with the Halsey family) had a store and Colon used to haul her groceries.

Nuecestown was once quite a little town. In 1861 there was one store there, owned by a man named Vetters. His wife was a sister of Bill McGregor. Others living there were Beynon, Wade, Orchard, a Baptist minister, old man George Reynolds, and Samuel Colon, who came to this country in 1854 and who owned some cattle at Nuecestown. When I lived there in 1861 there were no public schools, only private ones. My teacher was Horace Taylor, a large man who came from the North. He lived with his mother there, but

---

[26] He was referring to what we call Baffin Bay today.

[27] Gathering salt for trade was a major enterprise for the Corpus Christi area during the Civil War when the Union blockade shut off normal sources of supplies. Salt was a valuable commodity during the war.

after her death he married.[28] Later, he was a postmaster in Corpus Christi — I remember the little old red house where the post office was.

Another small community was Gussettville, on the other side of the Nueces in Live Oak County, not far from Fort Merrill. It was founded by Col. Gussett, who had a store there before he came to Corpus Christi to live. Gussettville had only a few houses, and most of its residents were Irish.

Mr. Gussett had been with Taylor's army in Mexico. In the war he was wounded in the hip, having a piece of his hip bone knocked off. He carried the piece of bone in his pocket and I saw it. I also saw a medal of merit given him for bravery and honor in 1847.[29] Mr. Gussett married Miss Margaret Evans, who was Welsh, whom I knew when she was a young lady.[30] They had a son, Norwick, who died in Corpus Christi when he was about 16 or 17 years old. They had another son, Horatio, and daughters Susie and Leona.[31]

It was in Col. Gussett's store in Corpus Christi, about 1866 or a little later, that I first met James Downing, who was clerking there. Bob Savage, Russell Savage's father, also worked in Gussett's store. Russell says he didn't, but I know better, he did. I knew him before Russell did.

When Corpus Christi was bombarded during the Civil War I was living at Nuecestown. I could hear the bombardment but didn't see it. As the Yankees were trying to get possession of all the boats they could, the Confederates dug a channel across the reef so as to take their boats up the river for safety.[32] One of the boats stuck and burned. They tried to get the channel dredge up the river, too, to

---

[28] Thomas Noakes taught at the Nuecestown school for a time; he borrowed the blackboard he had made for Horace Taylor. Noakes said in his diary he had 14 students in the fall class of 1865.

[29] Norwick Gussett was a first sergeant during the war and served under U.S. Grant and Robert E. Lee.

[30] Margaret Evans was born in Cardiff, Wales.

[31] There were six children in all. Norwick Jr. died from the bite of a brown recluse spider. Daughters married Royal Givens, C.J. McManus, George Reynolds, W. H. Brooks.

[32] The channel cut in the reef, to allow boats access to the Nueces River, was made in 1845 by Zachary Taylor's engineers.

keep it from falling into the Yankees' hands, but it stuck in the river. The Confederates got the lead off it to make bullets.

This channel they dug was not deep enough, in ordinary times, to interfere with travel across the reef along the line of stakes, but one time when Mr. Colon and I were taking some oxen across, it was from four and a half to five and a half feet deep because of a big rise in the river. We had to swim the oxen across the channel. It was in the middle of the reef then, not at this end, as it is now.

In 1862 much cotton was hauled by ox-carts and mule carts to Brownsville, as all other ports were blockaded. My brother William and I took two loads of cotton down there. Each of us had a wagon to drive, with four yoke of oxen, and I walked every step of the way from the King Ranch. Sometimes we didn't make more than four or five miles a day, but then again sometimes we made eight or nine. The roads in places were a mile wide, from so many mule and ox teams traveling them. The teams would keep getting off the sand on to the turf and it was pretty near all road.

We had a horse to hunt up the oxen each morning. The horse was usually tied behind the wagon as it moved along. One time old man McKenzie's lead horse was fastened behind the wagon, and he got stubborn and choked himself to death, and they dragged him a long time before they knew he was dead.

For huge mule teams you ought to have seen those that came in from Mexico in later years. There were frequently as many as 20 mules to one wagon. And the Chihuahua wagons — so-called because they came from Chihuahua — sometimes had as many as 30 mules hitched to one wagon and sometimes had two drivers. It took some time to hitch up that many mules and to turn them loose.

I left Mr. Colon in 1862 and worked for Mr. and Mrs. Holthaus, bakers in Corpus Christi, during the winter and spring of 1862 and 1863. It was during the Civil War and I remember I went to Victoria and got a hogshead of yellow sugar for the bakery, for cookies. Most people don't know what a hogshead is now. It was an enormous barrel and held hundreds of pounds of sugar, perhaps 500 pounds or more.

We had two large ox-carts for the trip. I drove one and a man named Long drove the other. The road wasn't very good and we had to ford all the rivers. One of these was the Guadalupe at Victoria. It was all I could do to keep on my feet, the current was so swift. Of course I walked alongside the oxen to drive them across. You had to whip them. That is the way to handle oxen. You had to control them with a whip.

When I was six years old I used to lead the lead ox on my father's farm when they ploughed his field, and when they turned the corners I was always glad of the chance to sit down and rest. The little fellows had to do their part in those days. They couldn't wait until they were grown to work, as they do now. We had to crawl before we walked.

It was hard for Mrs. Holthaus to get anyone to work for her, but I worked for her for six months and got along with her all right. I wasn't fired when I quit, either. That was the only time in my life I worked for a salary.

In the spring of 1863, when I was 16 years old, I quit the bakery and moved up to Casa Blanca. My father made arrangement for my brother William and myself to take charge of Belden and Gilpin's sheep. We were to have a share for our work.

Belden and Gilpin were partners in the Carmel Ranch[33] about three miles north of the old Casa Blanca on the Nueces River. They had sheep and horses. When Belden died, Judge Gilpin established a ranch on the Penitas Creek. He was a large man, a bachelor, and he remained at the Penitas Ranch until his death[34] in the ranch house there.

William and I went out to Belden and Gilpin's, but William stayed only one year. He quit and went off. That left it all on me. I stayed the three years out. William went to work for a man at a salary of $20 a month, and I was getting nothing. One time I didn't even have any clothes or shoes to wear.

---

[33] Frederick Belden named the ranch after his hometown of Carmel, N.Y. The Carmel Ranch was later sold to Cornelius Cox, who called it El Colimal, then later it was owned by Dean Miller.

[34] Belden died on March 18, 1867 in Corpus Christi and Gilpin died on Nov. 11, 1895 at his ranch. He died in poverty and in debt.

I went to work and dressed me some sheep skins and made me a pair of buckskin pants and some shoes, to have something to wear. I made them with my hands, sewed them with buck string. I had no needles and no thread, so I punched holes with an awl and ran the string in the holes and pulled it through. For a pattern I used an old pair of pants, and I cut it out with a knife.

Buckskin is dressed goatskin or sheepskin. You take the grain off first; that is what produces the hair or wool. You work that off with a bone, such as a horse's rib or a smooth stick. That leaves the inner part of the skin soft. You rub it with the new brains of an animal; rub the brains all over it and leave it on for a couple of days. Then wash it off clean. (You had to use your own brains to make the other brains valuable.) Then you get live-oak bark and bruise it and soak it in water. Put the buckskin in it. That dyes it and gives it a tan color.

A man named Murdock[35] would dye his buckskin by putting it up the chimney and smoking it. That made it dark-colored. This man was from the North. He was a ranch man and lived beyond the Oso. His son drowned in a hole.

Buckskin is warm until it gets wet. It absorbs water very easily. If it gets wet and a norther comes, you surely do get cold. I never saw a house for a year and was not inside a house for two years. The elements were my roof and the wilds were my house. I did my own cooking for four years and had nothing to eat but meat. I barbecued the meat, mostly. I had no bread and didn't know what a vegetable looked like. I didn't see people, sometimes, for months. My father would come once in a while to see how I was getting along. Harry, my brother, was there part of the time and I had to take care of him, too. I was 16 years old in March 1863 when I started out there. I took care of the sheep for three years and got 750 sheep out of it.

Later, my brother William and I went into partnership together in the sheep business and were together about 50 years.

---

[35] William Murdock was murdered on Aug. 19, 1872 when robbers tied him up and placed a heavy plow on his chest and set his house on fire.

After the Civil War we were troubled a lot with bandits. They captured me once, but didn't take me off. They came to my place and demanded two or three muttons, and I said, "Go ahead and take them." They took them and went out and barbecued them. I knew several of those in the party but I didn't let them know it, because I thought they might murder me if they did. I had no arms of any kind — never did out there at the sheep ranch.

These bandits were all Mexicans. They robbed and plundered considerably around here. There was a merchant train of ox wagons coming up from the Valley and I saw them rob that. A man named Stewart, who was a conscript officer during the war, was living at the Penitas Ranch. The bandits met him coming up the hill and murdered him right now. The bandits caught a Mexican and tied him up because he wouldn't take them to water, but he got away when they went to look for water. I went to sleep many nights not knowing whether I would be alive next morning or not. Another thing that bothered us a great deal out there was the wild lobo wolves. They were like police dogs, only larger. There were no panthers.

Some persons know very little of ranching life. Not long ago I was asked what a wallet was. A wallet was a rectangular-shaped pocket of cloth, the opening being down the middle of one of the pieces. You would put your cup, your coffee, and your clothes in it, or just anything and everything you wanted to, and hang it behind your saddle. Your cup was always a tin cup, and sometimes you would hang it on your saddle instead of putting it in your wallet.

It was in 1863 that I moved to Casa Blanca. My mother had died in Corpus Christi in March 1861. She is buried in old Bayview Cemetery, but there is nothing to mark the place. In those times they didn't have any marble slabs or monuments, and I don't even know exactly the place where she is buried. Her name was Mary Ann Anderson. In those days when they married they gave it out just three or four Sundays before the marriage was to take place. I guess my father and mother must have had a fuss, because when he went to be married she wasn't there. But they met up and made up again.

In the fall of 1866 my father and my youngest brother, John, returned to England. I believe my father went back to see my aunt, mother's sister. I reckon he thought he would get her and bring her over here, but he found she was already married. In December of 1867, he and John left England again for Texas, going to New York and taking the steamer *Raleigh* for Galveston. Twenty-one miles off the coast of Georgia the steamer caught fire and as the lifeboats were lowered they were swamped. I was informed that only 21 were saved. We never would have known what had become of my father and brother if it hadn't been that a friend of mine got a New York paper showing the list of passengers on that boat. In that way we knew they had sailed on that vessel and had been lost at sea.

I sometimes thought my father wished he had never come to this country. Many people came over here and made money, then went back and cursed this country. But they all came back. You know what the Frenchman said? "America is like a trap. You get into it, and if you ever get out, you get back into it again."

I was in Casa Blanca in 1867 when the yellow fever epidemic struck (Corpus Christi) and 67 people died from the fever.[36] The yellow fever in 1854 in Corpus Christi wasn't so bad; very few people died then.

I came to my present ranch site in 1869, my only move since I was married on Oct. 8, 1867 at Dodson Bend in Live Oak County. My wife's name was Eliza Lorena McWhorter. We had been married 67 years and seven months when she died on March 12, 1935, and had been given the blue ribbon for the oldest couple in Jim Wells County. Last year, on March 9, 1939, I celebrated my 92nd birthday with a chicken barbecue, in a grove of elm trees, all hung with moss, here on the place. It was attended by 145 people, mostly relatives.

People ask me how I managed to live to the ripe old age of 93 years. I ought to tell them it is because I was pickled when I was young, I was so thoroughly soaked with salty water. People

---

[36] Joseph Almond, who was living in Corpus Christi and kept a diary during the 1867 outbreak, listed 135 people who died of the fever, far fewer than most estimates but more than Adams' count.

nowadays take life too easy. If they want to go one block they will get in the car and ride. It reminds me of the man who walked three miles to get a horse to ride one mile. I always park my car when I go to Alice, then walk.

Robert Adams (1847-1944) (Plate 1) was born in England and arrived in Corpus Christi in 1852 with his immigrant parents, Mr. and Mrs. Robert Adams Sr., and his older brother William, when he was five years old. In the early years in Texas, Robert was a freighter's apprentice, hauled salt, and transported cotton down the Cotton Road during the Civil War. He was a sheepherder on shares and acquired his own flock of sheep and a ranch. In 1867, the brothers formed a partnership and began to raise sheep in what was then Nueces County and later became Jim Wells County. In 1878 they fenced their land and began to raise cattle. In 1893 the brothers divided their holdings and Robert kept the Tecolote Ranch, two miles west of Alfred. Robert married Lorena McWhorter in 1867. They had eight children. He was interviewed for his recollections "Learning by Hard Licks" by Marie Blucher from March 14, 1939 to Sept. 12, 1940. Robert Adams died on Aug. 26, 1944 when he was 97. Among those attending his funeral was his baby sister, Mary Ann Hinnant, who lived to be 108 before she died in 1964.

CHAPTER 2

WILLIAM ADAMS
RECOLLECTIONS

I came from England with my parents in 1852, being then six years old. We crossed the ocean on a sailing vessel, the voyage from Liverpool to New Orleans lasting seven weeks. From New Orleans an old black steamship called the *Mexico*[1] carried us to Galveston, whence we sailed to Indianola on a little old stern-wheel riverboat. From Indianola to Corpus Christi we were passengers on a little two-masted boat that carried the mail for years between those two points.

We landed in Corpus Christi in November 1852. Rube Holbein[2] met us at Ohler's Wharf when we landed. The wharf was in front of the block south of the Nueces Hotel (later). Holbein's father was Col. Kinney's agent in London. They advertised and sold land in 100-acre plots, with ten cows and calves. I remember that the ironwork front was being put on the Meuly house on Chaparral Street at the time we came. I think the Robertsons were already here. We lived near the Courthouse. The present courthouse grounds probably include the lot where we lived.

---

[1] A regular packet steamer operated by the Morgan Line from New Orleans to Galveston.

[2] Reuben Holbein was the son of John Holbein, Kinney's London agent. Reuben Holbein served in the Mexican War, in Mustang Gray's company, and later was the bookkeeper on the King Ranch.

Corpus Christi was a little ordinary place. It extended about as far as Artesian Square. There may have been one or two houses back up towards the hill, but not much was built up. It was quite a small place. On the bluff, in the present 400 block, Col. Kinney had a place where the present telephone building is located, this being the corner where Mrs. Atlee McCampbell lived before the telephone company brought the property. Next to that on the north was a brick house, that of Forbes Britton (Plate 13).[3]

The Ohler family — Mr. Edward Ohler, wife and two sons — had a house at the corner where the new post office is now being built. It was their home. They also had a two-story concrete house on the ground where the Nueces Hotel is now, or a little south of that, with a wharf out in front of the house.[4] The first school I went to was in that concrete building.

George Noessel lived on Chaparral Street. He was one of the principal merchants when we came here. Father Reilly[5] was the priest at that time. The first Methodist preacher was named Lafferty.[6] As to the schools of Corpus Christi in the early days, they were not much. A man named Craft[7] had the first school here that I remember. The first school I went to in Corpus Christi was in a house owned by Mrs. Murphy, in the Gussett block. People seem to have forgotten about it; there seemed to be some mystery about it. In the next block was the government mule yard. The government maintained headquarters[8] here when I came. They delivered freight to El Paso by mule team.

In the late 1850s the headquarters were moved to San Antonio. All of the young Englishmen that came over got employment with

---

[3] Still standing, known as the Centennial House.

[4] Edward Ohler arrived in 1848 with a stock of groceries and his family. His two-story shellcrete building was built in 1849 at the corner of Peoples and Water. Ohler's wharf extended into the bay from the foot of Peoples Street.

[5] Father Bernard O'Reilly.

[6] Rev. Henderson S. Lafferty organized the First Methodist Church in 1853.

[7] M. P. Craft was the principal of a school started by Charles Lovenskiold, which opened in the Ohler building on Water Street in 1853.

[8] Headquarters of the Eighth Military District were moved from San Antonio to Corpus Christi in 1853 and Army supplies were shipped from Corpus Christi to U.S. forts on the Texas frontier.

the government at $20 a month, and board, driving a mule team. There were a wagon master and a teamster to each six-mule wagon, and frequently from 10 to 30 wagons in a train.

The place known in later years as the Doddridge home was originally the Schatzell home. Mr. Schatzell[9] had a little bunch of cattle and used the brand STS. He died in 1852. Capt. Fullerton was Schatzell's administrator.

After Mrs. Fullerton's death, Capt. Fullerton married his wife's sister. One of the two daughters died; and the other, Rachel, married Perry Doddridge (Plate 20). Mr. and Mrs. Doddridge lived at the old Schatzell place until their deaths. The property was left to the Presbyterian Church, and the old house was later torn down to make way for the Doddridge Memorial Building of the Presbyterian Church.

Some time between 1852 and 1854 I saw them dig the foundation for the Catholic church. They made a concrete foundation, but the building was of timber.[10]

There were two very prominent men here at that time. One was Forbes Britton,[11] who lived at Britton Motts, several miles in the country. The other was Judge Webb,[12] who lived at the place now called Avery Point.[13] This place should have been named Webb Point, as the judge improved it extensively, building houses and barns. He had three or four fields. The fences around them had posts of ebony. He owned a great many Negroes. Judge Webb was a district judge. One of his daughters married Colonel Kinney; they

---

[9] John Peter Schatzell lived in "Mansion House," later known as the Fullerton house and the Doddridge house. Schatzell was a wealthy merchant in Matamoros who retired to Corpus Christi. He died on Oct. 24, 1854.

[10] Rev. Bernard O'Reilly built the first Catholic church on Tancahua, between Antelope and Leopard.

[11] Forbes Britton, merchant, state senator and Mexican War veteran.

[12] James Webb served as secretary of Treasury, secretary of state, and attorney general of the Republic of Texas. He moved to Corpus Christi after his daughter Mary Elizabeth married Henry Kinney and he was appointed judge of the 14th Judicial District. Webb County (Laredo) was named for him.

[13] Where Judge Webb lived is now known as the Avery Point Turning Basin of the Port of Corpus Christi.

were later separated. We lived near the Webbs for about six or seven years, being engaged in farming in a small way.

This was beautiful country between the creeks. From the Oso to Agua Dulce it was a beautiful prairie, there being no timber except on the creeks. On the Oso mesquite trees were to be found, the only place they grew. All the way up to the Agua Dulce, and nearly to San Diego, also, the country was particularly beautiful, still a prairie country without timber, except on the creeks, where hackberry and live oak trees were to be found.

As to Indians, it was reported along in 1853 that there was a bunch of Indians around here. I don't know. We lived at Avery Point for a number of years and never did meet any Indians. We didn't use to think anything of saddling up a horse and getting a wallet, cup and blanket, and wherever night came you would unsaddle and sleep. I have slept out many a night, using my saddle for a pillow. The coyotes would chew your rope in two just for meanness. There were many rattlesnakes, but I don't recollect any of our family — and there are a great many of us — ever having been snake-bit.

During the Civil War, the Yankees came here and demanded the surrender of Corpus Christi,[14] but the people in town didn't do it. They were given 24 hours to move families out. The women and children were taken for safety out in the country, to the motts in various places, which gave some shelter.

The bombardment commenced early in the morning before daylight (Plate 4). About two o'clock in the afternoon another boy and myself walked in to town. We went down on the beach in front of the courthouse, where there was an 18-pounder cannon, an old cast cannon. Major Felix Blucher[15] was there. A Yankee ship out in the bay looked as if it were right opposite. Mr. Blucher said, "I believe I'll take a pop at it." And he sighted, and he took a pop and

[14] Lt. John W. Kittredge, commander of Union warships blockading the Aransas Pass channel, led the attack on Corpus Christi with a flotilla of shallow-draft warships in August 1862.

[15] Maj. Felix von Blucher, a civil engineer and surveyor, served as major of engineers and captain of artillery for Confederate forces in Texas. He established his home in Corpus Christi in 1849.

it looked like the bullet hit the water to the right side of the ship. So he said, "I believe I'll take another one," and he did. The ship was broadside. We never saw the shell hit the water; and the ship got up and moved from there, and we were satisfied that we hit her.

A week or two afterwards, they captured eight or ten Yankees, and I heard them say that the shell struck the stern of the ship[16] and came very near going to the magazine. It was Capt. Kittredge's ship. There was not a company of soldiers present when this shot was fired, only Major Blucher and two or three others. There were two 18-pounder cannon on the hill. A young man named Billy Mann moved them down on the beach in the night, before they commenced bombarding. Only one man was killed on the Confederate side.

In front of the courthouse there was a bank or slope and a company was stationed there. The Yankees landed in the Rincon[17] with a small cannon and started down to where our troops were. We had a company of cavalry in the gully back here and they were sent up against the Yankees. The steamer got aground or they would have killed a lot of them. Grapeshot was fired all around.

A friend living up in Live Oak County was down here some time afterwards and he picked up a shell about 10 or 18 inches long. We took it to his home where it lay around in the yard for years. Finally his wife used it to rest the wash boiler on while heating the water for the washing and it exploded. These friends were the Shipps.

When the Yankees came to the mouth of the Rio Grande, Gen. Bee[18] was in command of Confederate troops in Brownsville. Gen. Bee used to live in Corpus on the corner where Mrs. Atlee McCampbell lived recently. Bee later went to San Antonio. At this time Brownsville was the only outlet in Texas for the thousands and thousands of bales of cotton hauled here from Arkansas and other

---

[16] The ship fired on by Maj. Felix Blucher was the *Corypheus*.

[17] Later known as North Beach.

[18] Gen. Hamilton P. Bee, in charge of Confederate forces in South Texas, was a legislator and businessman before the war. Bee County was named for his father, Brig. Gen. Bernard E. Bee, secretary of war during the Texas Revolution.

states. Gen. Bee moved all of the cotton from this side of the river to the Mexican side.

You would be surprised at the big lots of cotton and the number of wagons hauling it. Once, Gen. Bee burned all the cotton between Brownsville and the Santa Gertrudis so the Yankees wouldn't get it. When the Yankees moved to Brownsville,[19] the cotton was diverted to Rio Grande City. I drove an ox wagon from Banquete to Rio Grande City in 1864 loaded with cotton.

When the Yankees got to Rio Grande City, the cotton was diverted to Laredo and hauled down the river on the Mexican side to Brownsville. The price of cotton went as high as $1 a pound. I drove wagons loaded with cotton from Laredo to Brownsville in 1864, receiving $10 a month.

At one time Corpus Christi was the biggest wool port in the United States. Most of the wool was from Mexico. In those days it was not unusual to have as many as six killings a week on the Hill. John Dunn, one of the finest men I knew, played a brave part through all the dangers of pioneering. He was an eighth son; after him was born a girl. Now all are dead but John. He has six daughters, but no sons.

Sally Sculle[20] was quite a character. Her first husband was Jesse Robertson.[21] The Robertsons of Live Oak County are her descendants. She carried a pistol and rode like a man. Taking a Mexican along, she would buy cattle all the way between here and the Rio Grande and sell them to people. She also traded in horses. Charles Stillman[22] was here during the Mexican War. He owned the

---

[19] Union invasion forces under the command of Gen. Nathaniel P. Banks captured Brownsville in the first week of November 1863 and moved up the coast, capturing Confederate forts on the barrier islands, including Fort Semmes on Mustang Island and Fort Esperanza on Matagorda Island.

[20] Usually spelled Skull. Her real name was Sarah Jane Newman.

[21] Her first husband was Jesse Robinson, not Robertson, and her second husband was George Scull, who disappeared. She kept his name, changing the spelling to Skull.

[22] Charles Stillman, a merchant in Matamoros and Brownsville, was an early partner of Richard King and Mifflin Kenedy. He bought disputed land claims throughout South Texas. From traffic in cotton during the Civil War, he became

Laureles Ranch, which was managed for him by a Canadian named Gregory.[23]

In 1863 I moved to Alice. I was county commissioner of Nueces County for 16 years. Nueces County was organized in 1846. I knew the first sheriff, the first county judge, and two of the first county commissioners. The reason I didn't know the other two was that one lived in Laredo and one in Brownsville. The county line followed the Rio Grande from Laredo down to Brownsville and then up the Gulf Coast to Corpus Christi.

———

William Adams (1846-1939) (Plate 3) was born in Norfolk, England. He came to Texas with his parents, Robert and Sarah (Anderson) Adams Sr. when he was six. He freighted cotton on the Cotton Road during the Civil War and started a sheep ranch with his brother Robert after the war. After he and his brother ended their ranching partnership, he started his own ranch near Alice in 1891. For 16 years, he was a county commissioner of Nueces County. He helped organize Jim Wells County in 1912 and served as ex officio county judge for a time. He married Sarah Dodson in January 1867 and after her death in 1894 he married Nina Young. He was the father of seven children. Date of interview by Marie Blucher — Dec. 14, 1938 at the home of his daughter, Mrs. A. M. French, in Corpus Christi. Mr. Adams was 93 years old at the time. He died on Jan. 12, 1939 after a stroke. Before his death, the city of Alice paid a tribute to Mr. Adams by naming the high school the William Adams High School.

---

one of the wealthiest men in the country and after the war he moved to New York City, where he died in 1875.

[23] William S. Gregory, who also served as county commissioner in the late 1850s.

CHAPTER 3

ANDREW ANDERSON
REMINISCENCES

To refresh the writer's memory of an old Dutch windmill that stood on the east side of the block on which the Nueces Hotel is now located, he went about to find a photograph which would now be quite in contrast with the shoreline of Corpus Christi. The only person who might have a clue to such a photograph was Captain Anderson, so the writer (E. L. Caldwell) took the matter up with him. This led to a very interesting account of his early experiences in Corpus Christi which were greatly at variance with present-day circumstances.

Captain Andy Anderson relates that his father, Captain John Anderson, came to this country from Stockholm, Sweden, and for a time lived in New Orleans. At the time of the Mexican War he had several schooners and entered into the business of carrying freight and soldiers from New Orleans to Corpus Christi. His first trip was in the 1840s.[1] He may have decided to build here as early as that, but he did not until he settled here about 1851. He built a house just where the old Dutch windmill (Plate 5) stood for so long a time and then returned to New Orleans to get his family.

---

[1] Units of Zachary Taylor's army began landing on North Beach on July 31, 1845 and continued to concentrate at Corpus Christi until the army left for the Rio Grande in March 1846.

At the time Taylor's army was camped in Corpus Christi on the way to Mexico, Captain John Anderson brought supplies to them by schooner from New Orleans. At that time there were no wharves or landing spots on the shore for the schooners and sloops drawing as much as six feet of water, so these boats would come up to shore about where the Breakers Hotel now is[2] and then the freight was carried to shore in small boats or skiffs.

Captain Anderson began building a brick house made of shell and lime on the lot now occupied by the rear of the Palace Theater and Scogin's garage. At that time there had been several other houses built of similar material. The lime for the bricks or blocks was made by digging a large hole in the ground and lining it with oyster shells, which were then burned. This lime held the shells together in the blocks.

He finished his house before going back to New Orleans for his family. He then brought his wife, a son, Captain Andy Anderson, and a step-son, Chris Yung. Captain Andy Anderson was born in New Orleans in 1852, but John and Will, his brothers, Mrs. Lillie Rankin, and Mrs. Amanda J. Keller, sisters, were born in Corpus Christi. (Old records in La Retama Library show that Chris Young used C. W. Yung as his signature. This was perhaps derived from his father's name, which was either German or Swedish.)

Later on a man by the name of W. H. Berry[3] used the clay on the south end of the bluff to make brick. Up to the time of the 1919 storm there were remnants of this brick kiln on the block in front of Caldwell and Born properties at the end of South Broadway. Some have said Berry's red brick, being soft, fell to pieces easily, yet Bill Grant's house built of those red bricks stood on the corner of Water Street just south of the Nueces Hotel until the hurricane of 1919.

Another house of shell and lime blocks was built by a Mr. Kelly and was located near the Courthouse.[4] The old Meuly house on

---

[2] Off North Beach.

[3] Henry W. Berry, early builder with J.A.F. Gravis, and first sheriff of Nueces County.

[4] This was the house built by Martin Kelly. A description of this house is included in the chapter on Annie Marie Kelly.

Chaparral and the Cahill house[5] just back of it facing Water were quite elaborate houses of the same material. These were plastered over with cement made from the lime, and although the Cahill house was destroyed during the 1919 storm, the old Meuly house still stands.[6] There was a house built earlier than any of these which was built by Belden and associates and is reported to have been used as a warehouse for Taylor's army.

An old landmark in Captain Andy's Anderson's mind is the Evans place built of shell concrete at 411 North Broadway. This is in its original state with only moderate repairs (Plate 13).[7] Such were the buildings and outstanding points of interest according to Captain Andy Anderson's recollection. The old Dutch windmill did not come into existence until quite some time later (Plate 7).

Among slave-holders in Corpus Christi were Mr. Johnson, Mr. Moore, Mr. Gravis and Mr. Edward Ohler. Mr. Ohler had two sons, William and Charles. The Ohlers lived over their store.[8] They had three women slaves and two men slaves. Mrs. Ohler[9] would sit on the porch upstairs and ring her bell when she wanted a slave to come. Old Rachel, one of the slaves, stole some silver, which was found under her mattress, and she was sentenced to receive 25 lashes at the whipping post. This post was back of where the city hall is now.[10] The constable came and got Rachel to take her to be whipped. He put a strong strap around her waist and led her away. I followed in a crowd of little boys who tagged along behind. The constable tied Rachel very strongly to the post. We boys sat around

---

[5] The two-story Cahill House across from Central Wharf, on Water Street, was also built by Henry W. Berry. It was damaged during the 1919 storm and demolished soon afterwards (Plate 14).

[6] Conrad Meuly's two-story home on Chaparral, built of shellcrete, had walls two feet thick, rooms with 14-foot ceilings and the front was decorated with iron grillwork from New Orleans. It was torn down in 1955.

[7] This was the house built by Forbes Britton, about 1850, known as Centennial House today, and is still standing.

[8] Edward Ohler arrived in 1848 and began a grocery business. His two-story shellcrete building was built in 1849 at the corner of Peoples and Water. The Ohlers later built a new home on the bluff.

[9] Matilda Ohler and Henry Kinney were conducting an indiscreet love affair.

[10] Market Square, between Peoples and Schatzell on Mesquite.

in a circle. The constable pulled out his long whip and gave her the 25 lashes. With each blow of the whip she would give a big jerk. Mr. Ohler paid $500 for a Negro boy about 15 years old. He was bought from a man who had lots of slaves, in Matagorda.

Andy Anderson went to school with Father Gonnard.[11] Father Gonnard, a priest, was principal of a Catholic school on the bluff. It was in a little brick house called the Parker place, which was about a block south of where the convent is now. Mr. Carroll and Mr. Campion[12] were teachers in this school.

Mr. and Mrs. Carpenter had a school for boys and girls, having at times as many as a hundred scholars. This was held on the bluff in the old Chapman house, but at that time it was located on what is now South Broadway, approximately where the Hirsch home now stands. The rules of conduct were framed and hanging up just inside the door. Mr. Carpenter did not whip or slap anybody. If a pupil would not obey the rules, he had to go home.

During the Civil War, the Yankees sought to establish their headquarters at Aransas Pass, which at that time was a very small settlement.[13] When the Confederates perceived what the Yankees had in mind they attempted to blow up the lighthouse. (The lighthouse, built in 1855, still stands.)[14] The Confederates did not succeed so the Yankees repaired it and landed at Aransas Pass where they established a garrison of three regiments. They had many cannons which they set up in the sand hills.

The Yankees went around the bay and commandeered all the boats they could find. The people of Corpus Christi burned two sloops rather than let them fall into Yankee hands. Two of the larger craft started full sail toward the location of Portland and another tried to go up the Nueces Bay but grounded on a reef. The

---

[11] Father John Gonnard, a Catholic priest from France. After he died in the yellow fever epidemic of 1867, the school was operated by Father Berthet.

[12] William Campion and William Carroll. Carroll's niece later became superintendent of schools and a high school was named for her, the Mary Carroll High School. William's brother and Mary Carroll's father was the architect and builder, Charles Carroll.

[13] The settlement by the Aransas Pass channel is today's Port Aransas.

[14] The Aransas Pass Lighthouse on Harbor Island.

hands on board burned her. Many of the lighter draft boats succeeded in getting up the river and away.[15]

The Yankees took after the ones bound for the north side of the bay where Portland now is. A boat named *Breakers* was manned by a Russian called Sam and old Jack Hardin, who for many years was a pilot at Port Aransas. Upon seeing that the Yankees were overtaking them and that escape was impossible, they hastily got provisions together to abandon ship. Before leaving they planned to blow her up. It seems that some of their provisions were in identical sacks as the gunpowder. Excitedly, they lifted the lids off the stove in the galley in which a fire was burning, threw in what they thought was a sack of gunpowder, then dived and swam for shore. They expected the explosion to come at any minute, but to their surprise when they got ashore and looked back they saw the Yankees boarding her. They simply could not imagine why the boat had not blown up. Their wonder was short-lived for when they began to prepare a meal, Russian Sam opened the sack of coffee and exclaimed, "My God! Jack, we've got the gunpowder instead of the coffee!"

The Yankees got the *Breakers* and the sloop *Hannah* was burned near the beach somewhere near where the Princess Louise Hotel is now located. At that time there was a great high shell beach there. The *Hannah* was owned by Captain Jack Sands, who had only one eye. The *Augusta*, a sloop, and the *AB*, a sternwheeler, managed to get out of range up the Nueces River. These two boats took only three feet of water and the Nueces Bay was about seven feet deep then. The *Reindeer* escaped by going out to sea. It drew too much water to go up the river. Later it was wrecked outside the bar at Aransas Pass.[16] Some say the remains of the old *Reindeer* can be seen way up north of the pass. When the water is clear the

---

[15] Capt. Anderson's chronology is flawed. The Union capture of Fort Semmes on Mustang Island followed the invasion by Union forces in November 1863. The action of chasing shallow-draft boats on the bay happened a year earlier, during Capt. Kittredge's attack on Corpus Christi in August 1862.

[16] The schooner *Reindeer* did not escape by going to sea. It was captured on July 9, 1862 and used by Lt. Kittredge in the attack on Corpus Christi. The ship wrecked in February 1870.

timbers can be seen below the surface. The *AB* was abandoned about where old Nuecestown was located. Until recently the old boiler could still be seen on the land about 150 to 250 feet from the Nueces River.

The *Admiral Foote*, another small Confederate steamer, is also remembered by Captain Anderson. This boat was lost at Aransas Pass in a wreck about 1868 or 1869. *Elmer*, a schooner, burned on the bar between Corpus Christi and Nueces Bay, at what was known as the reef. The *Belle Italia*, a Confederate boat owned by someone in Lamar, was captured by the Yankees.[17] It is the sloop referred to later as sighting a cannon on the little group at Flour Bluff.

Although Captain Anderson was only about 10 years old at this time, he remembers much of the excitement and gossip, no doubt confirmed in his memory by hearing it over and over again.

There were several Indians in the Confederate troops. They could speak good English. "One nearly scared the life out of me once. A group of Confederates were camped not far from our house and I used to go to the camp nearly every day. Their camp was in the backyard of a long old house with a long gallery which stood at a point opposite of the present location of the Nueces Hotel on the south. I used to be good at gigging fish. One day one of the Indian soldiers borrowed my gig and began throwing it towards my foot, each time striking the ground just an inch or two from my toe. He certainly had me dancing around."

While the Yankees were threatening to occupy Corpus Christi, there was a Frenchman and his wife marooned here who were so anxious to get out of the line of battle they promised Captain John Anderson $150 to take them in his sloop, the *White Pelican,* with their luggage to Peñascal. This was about 60 miles down the lagoon in Kenedy's pasture and was little more than the location of a store which was run by the Morton brothers. At that time there was an

---

[17] Along with the *Reindeer*, the *Belle Italia* was captured at Lamar, with a cargo of corn and bacon, by Lt. Kittredge in July 1862. He added the *Reindeer* and *Belle Italia* to his shallow-draft fleet in the attack on Corpus Christi in August 1862.

ox-cart road from Peñascal to Brownsville and after reaching Peñascal they could go by land to Brownsville and from there by water to New Orleans.

Captain Anderson agreed to take them but before they reached Flour Bluff they were overtaken and captured by the Yankees at Shamrock[18] and then taken to Aransas Pass. Shamrock Point was on Mustang Island right across the bay from here. The Yankees came out of the cove while Anderson's boat was sailing around the outside of the cove. At Aransas Pass[19] the major[20] made arrangements to send the Frenchman and his wife on to New Orleans to their great relief.

Captain Anderson asked to be allowed to come back to Corpus Christi and after holding him a day and a night they agreed to let him go. The major inquired of him as to the supply of provisions, sugar and coffee, in Corpus Christi and being told that provisions were short the major commanded that his sloop be well stocked with supplies for the people in Corpus Christi and on the mainland. Upon Captain John Anderson's arrival in Corpus Christi neither the supplies were well-received nor his intentions in bringing them well-considered. Many of the citizens refused to accept any of the provisions and they could not be prevailed upon in any manner to do so.

Of course, news from the outside was very rare during the blockade days and Captain Anderson succeeded in bringing back from Aransas Pass some Northern newspapers. These papers were passed from hand to hand until they were worn out and the print rubbed off.

Some of the Confederate soldiers, while in a state of drunkenness, fell to discussing the Yankee major's kindness to Captain Anderson and came to the conclusion that Captain Anderson was a spy and should be hanged. They were overheard by

---

[18] Shamrock Island off Mustang Island.

[19] The ship channel, not the later town.

[20] Maj. William Thompson commanded 20th Iowa soldiers left to garrison Fort Semmes, which they renamed Post Aransas.

a friend of Anderson's, Bill Tinney,[21] who came straightway to Anderson's house to warn him. Captain Anderson got away by boat and went back to Aransas Pass. Here he explained the situation to the very surprised Yankee major. The major then said since such was the case Anderson should stay at Aransas Pass and pilot the Yankee ships in and out of the bay. He worked in this capacity at Aransas Pass for two years.

During the time Captain John Anderson piloted the Yankee boats around these coastal waters he sometimes made secret trips, at his own risk, across the bay to visit his family. He was often accompanied by some of the Yankee soldiers. One night, he awoke and saw guns stacked up in the yard, and the blue coats of Yankee boys moving around. It was not unusual for these visitors to go around in town a little, and although there was a small encampment of Confederate troops up on the bluff, no encounter was known to have taken place. (The Confederate soldiers were mostly just cowboys.)

It was during this time that the Yankees decided on the bombardment of Corpus Christi.[22] They gathered their fleet together and sailed into the bay flying a white flag. Old Major Gilpin, a rancher from Banquete, went out to Ohler's Wharf, where Peoples Street now is, with the flag of truce, a handkerchief tied on a stick. He was told that the town was to be bombarded at 10 o'clock the next morning and ordered them to have women and children evacuated. None of Mr. Gilpin's descendants are known to be living in Corpus Christi at this time.[23]

The inhabitants left the town in all kinds of vehicles and on foot after having first buried what they could to keep the Yankees from finding it. They threw up tents and tried to make the best of it but food was scarce, the only available water was in ponds and they

---

[21] One of the Tinney girls later married John Anderson's stepson, Chris Yung.

[22] Captain Andy Anderson's chronology of events must be wrong, since the bombardment occurred in 1862 more than a year before Union troops captured and occupied the fort on Mustang Island.

[23] Henry Gilpin, Frederick Belden's business and ranching partner, came to Corpus Christi in the 1840's; he was a lifelong bachelor (See Chapter 7).

were persecuted by mosquitoes. Captain Andy Anderson was on the wharf at the time the Yankees came into the bay and saw old gray-haired Major Gilpin go to meet the federal officer.[24] For safety the Anderson family went to Flour Bluff in an ox-wagon, staying in an old house they had there which they used to store salt handled in their big salt business. Others at Flour Bluff were the Golds, who had gone out with the Andersons, and the Singers,[25] who lived there, being engaged in the salt business also and who had their own salt shed.

One Sunday morning, probably Aug. 17, 1862, while the Andersons were staying at Flour Bluff, the *Belle Italia* with a six-foot cannon mounted on her bow came to the Point. They sighted the cannon on the Bluff and the crowd that was watching immediately scattered, but returned when Capt. Kittredge came ashore and waved his hat, telling them to stop, that they weren't going to shoot anyone.

Kittredge inquired as to how the families were faring for food. They told him they had fish, corn and molasses they got for the use of one of their boats. It was Russian Sam who was using the boat. He would make trips up to Matagorda and Caney Creek.

The captain sent back to the sloop and had provisions brought back consisting of crackers, bacon and coffee. He noticed an old man sitting on a white horse listening to the conversation. He approached this man and told him that it had been a long time since he had ridden a horse and that he would like to take a ride. The old man, a Mr. Priest, was somewhat reluctant, saying that he had a long way to go before dark. Captain Kittredge had him and another old man by the name of Gold put into the small boat under guard and taken out to the sloop, with orders to keep them there until he returned.

He overlooked another old man some distance from the crowd, perhaps because he was utterly disconsolate and all slumped down,

---

[24] Lt. John W. Kittredge, commanded the bark *Arthur* blockading the Aransas Pass channel.

[25] John Singer, whose brother Merritt invented the sewing machine, moved his family from their place on the southern end of Padre Island to Flour Bluff for safety at the beginning of the war.

having figured that the worst had come. This unimportant old man turned out to be, as you will learn later, the downfall of Captain Kittredge. When Captain Kittredge returned from his ride he turned the horse's reins over to Capt. Andy Anderson, who was just a small boy, and told him to take care of the horse as he would be back soon. This important news was overheard by the old man who had been unnoticed, and as quickly as possible he made his way to Corpus Christi and reported to the Confederates.

The Confederates plotted to ambush Kittredge by waiting for him in a house at Flour Bluff belonging to the man by the name of Priest. In about 10 days' time the sloop returned and about 21 soldiers (all there were aboard with the exception of one man) came ashore. Anderson, a boy, was on the wharf fishing but the Yankees did not molest him. They leaned their rifles in a stack and started pulling off their coats, saying that they were going out to hunt meat, as their supplies were low.

While thus disarmed they were surrounded by the Confederates who had been concealed in the old house on the landing. Captain Kittredge turned over his gun to the Confederate officer and surrendered. These Yankee prisoners were marched to town and then to San Antonio, where they were later paroled and sent home.[26] Captain Kittredge was quite a young fellow and he seemed very nice. It is said that after the war he engaged in the real estate business in Houston.

During the occupancy of the island by the federal soldiers, an unfortunate incident occurred. With the intention of arriving at Aransas Pass a boat of federal soldiers came to Corpus Pass by mistake. There they embarked in their launches to enter the Pass, presumably to locate the federal army. At the time the Confederates occupied the north end of Padre Island and there were a few soldiers stationed there. As the launches entered the pass, the Confederates on the big hill some 40 or 50 feet high could look down into the boats and shoot the soldiers. There must have been much bitterness by the Confederates because the federals were

---

[26] Lt. John W. Kittredge rejoined the war, but he was later court-martialed and discharged for striking an ordinary seaman.

helpless and made every effort to make them understand that they would surrender. But little attention was given this and a number of federals were killed and the others were captured.[27]

Some of the captured men were brought up to the Anderson bathhouse on the wharf in front of the old home.[28] The name of one recalled was Peter Baxter, who had a great ring on his finger. He said they had wanted to surrender but were not allowed to. He died from his wounds and was buried somewhere in Corpus Christi, probably in the old Bayview Cemetery. (The west of the cemetery, all along that side, was lined with graves of Negro soldiers.)

These launches were finally brought up to Corpus Christi full of holes and lay on the beach for a long time. Captain Anderson remembers plugging up the holes and trying to use the boats.

Later, when the Yankees evacuated Aransas Pass, Captain John Anderson was ordered to pilot the ships to Brownsville. From Brownsville he went to New Orleans where he was ordered to take charge of the steamer *Planter* full of Negro troops — three regiments, consisting of 700 or 800 men — and to land them at Corpus Christi.[29]

These Negro troops were here six months and were moved out by detachments until only one regiment remained. Major White, Lt. Downing, Major E. J. Nickerson, Lt. E. H. Wheeler were the white officers in command of the troops. It is interesting to note that these men settled in Corpus Christi and married in the community. Lt. Downing[30] married Miss Mary Blucher. In recalling Major Nickerson, it is said he did not stand socially very high. He lived up the Nueces River and built quite a house overlooking the river close

---

[27] Three Union sailors were killed in the skirmish at Corpus Christi Pass on Dec. 7, 1862. Confederate officers involved in the fight were Capt. H. Willke and Capt. John Ireland, later a governor of Texas.

[28] On Water Street.

[29] Gen. Phil Sheridan, who took possession of Texas for the Union at the end of the war, ordered the 25th Army Corps to occupy Galveston, Indianola, Brownsville and Corpus Christi. Some 52,000 Union troops were stationed along the coast, out of 70,000 in the state.

[30] Lt. James Downing married Mary Blucher, daughter of Felix and Maria von Blucher, on Nov. 16, 1867.

to where the Robstown Pump House[31] now stands. At that time Captain Andy Anderson carried on the old *Flour Bluff* (Plate 8), which was then about 50 feet long, a large amount of lumber for this house. The other officers referred to — Major White, Lt. Wheeler, Lt. Downing — moved in the best social circles in town. Lt. Wheeler later married Elizabeth McCampbell and Major White married Fannie Mallory.

Idleness is often the devil's workshop, and there came a time when the Negroes[32] cut up considerably. One of them frightened a Mrs. Staples with a controversy over the water from the cement cisterns. The Negro pushed her off the cistern. As a result of this, a mob spirit among the citizens rose against the Negroes. The major called a town meeting, and after negotiations with the officers it was agreed that they should be removed. Dad Grant[33] (later Captain Andy Anderson's father-in-law) was employed to transport the Negroes to Point Isabel, and they were loaded on his boat, the sloop *May*. On the voyage a storm blew up not far from Point Isabel and the boat was in such danger that she was beached, but the troops were saved and marched by land to their destination. This was the last of the Civil War as far as Corpus Christi was concerned.

In the 1870s, Captain Andy Anderson was carrying freight from Corpus Christi up the Nueces River to Sharpsburg[34] on the schooner *Flour Bluff*. While coming up the river one day in 1875 he got stuck on the mud and from there could see the old Noakes' place which had been burned during the night.[35] Later, arriving at the bahk of the river below the old store, he found the Noakes family cooking breakfast. He well remembers that they had one small pot held over the fire with three sticks. They told him of the Mexican raid and

---

[31] I think he must mean the original water pumping plant on the Nueces River at Calallen.

[32] The occupation troops.

[33] Capt. James Grant, a native of Halifax, Nova Scotia.

[34] Sharpsburg, northwest of Nuecestown, was just above Borden's Ferry on the north side Nueces River in San Patricio County.

[35] This was the Nuecestown Raid, sometimes called the Noakes Raid, during the Easter weekend of 1875.

how Mr. Noakes[36] had escaped through the cellar under the house and from there through a tunnel out to the river bank, the rest of the family having already abandoned the place. While he was there Sidney Borden[37] came in. The bandits had just taken from him his white horse and his watch. He told them that when he could get back to Corpus Christi he was going "plumb to the City of Mexico after them."

Soon after the Civil War a schooner, *W. H. McCauley*, with a captain named Mr. Hubbard came to Corpus Christi Pass by mistake. The bill of lading, the captain said, called for Corpus Christi and he did not know of any other way to get here except through Corpus Pass, as he had never heard of Aransas Pass. However, he found no light and no pilot, but the Gulf was smooth and from the bar looked satisfactory. He came in first with his small boat to examine the crossing and found about ten and a half feet of water across the bar. He could see a good channel 12 to 14 feet deep and quite ample for coming through. But when he reached about halfway through the Pass and down toward what is called the Bulk Head, which connects the island with Flour Bluff, the pass was only about seven feet deep and his schooner drew nine feet. From where this halted him he could see Corpus Christi through his glasses from the mast.

He came up to Corpus Christi in his yawl and went directly to the Customs House where J. W. Ward was customs officer, quite a gruff old fellow. He asked Captain Hubbard why he was trying to come in through Corpus Christi Pass. "Well, I thought I had to come to Corpus Christi through that pass," was the reply. "I did not know there was an Aransas Pass."

It was later arranged for John Anderson and others to go out and lighter the boat and finally bring it to Corpus. While the schooner was held at Corpus Pass a thunderstorm came up and one of her masts was shattered with lightning. After the schooner was

---

[36] Thomas J. Noakes, an English immigrant, operated a store at Nuecestown.
[37] Sidney Borden, founder of Sharpsburg, was the cousin of Gail Borden, the inventor of canned milk.

lightered she was brought to Corpus Christi, where it was difficult to secure a new mast.

Time now seems important, but in those years the time to put up a new mast was important enough to take months. Mr. Curry volunteered to furnish the mast and so we went down to Corpus Christi Pass and along the beach[38] picked up the proper material and brought it to Corpus where it was dressed to size and shape; before it was finished it was discovered to have a rotten defect. Now, Mr. Curry said he had another in sight at the Pass, and so after about a month returned with better material, and finally the mast was completed. After this great loss of time the schooner was re-rigged and left with hides and wool for New York. It had come from New York with a load of freight.

After the Civil War, and perhaps as late as 1872 to 1875, when Captain Anderson was about 20 years old, the old Dutch windmill (Plate 7) was built on the site originally referred to. The idea of this mill, of course, was brought to this country from Sweden. It was the first power plant at Corpus Christi and was used to saw wood and grind corn.

Looking back now, this would appear to be a minor matter but in those days both were important. Not much corn was grown, just enough to care for the needs of the community. The meal that was ground by the Anderson mill was good meal. Somewhat later the mill was used for grinding salt also, as it was noticed that much of the salt being gathered was too coarse for convenient use. A sugar roller was obtained and supported across an open box, with a hopper above, from which the salt lumps were fed. The size of the ground salt was controlled by loosening or tightening the rollers.

The business of getting wood was a real problem, as there was little wood anywhere except up the Nueces River and some on the north side of Nueces Bay. Captain Andy Anderson with one of his schooners built in 1860 by Captain John Anderson brought down wood from the Nueces River and from White's Point.[39] This was unloaded at a little wharf in front of where the big windmill was

---

[38] Mahogany logs often washed ashore on Padre Island.
[39] On the north side of Nueces Bay.

located. In going up the river as far as Nuecestown to Sharpsburg, the river at that time permitted a draft of about seven feet of water. Until the 1919 storm, Captain Anderson had the records of the wood ordered and the customers to whom it was sold, together with many records which no doubt would include many names familiar to old-timers. The old schooner was called the *Flour Bluff* (Plate 8). She went through the war and ran the blockade from Indianola and by Aransas Pass and down as far as Peñascal.

Captain Andy Anderson has a picture showing the *Flour Bluff* remodeled with three masts and on the back of it written by himself is the following: "First built in 1860 by Captain John Anderson. Through the Civil War. Rebuilt in 1879, lengthened 12 feet. Rebuilt in 1900, lengthened 20 feet. Made three masts. Lost in 1919 storm. Captain Andy Anderson owner."

White's Point is the designation we used in the early days. The name was not White Point, as asserted by some, but White's Point, the name being given to the locality because the White family[40] lived there and had taken a large part in its activities. (This is verified by the statements of C. F. H. V. Blucher in the past, he having been well-informed about the people and traditions of early days.)

Marking the present location of Sharpsburg now one finds nothing but two big palms. Go out Highway 9 a mile or two beyond the Nueces River bridge and turn north. The only marks remaining of the old store of Borden's are some old farming implements lying around close by. The site is given as being from two to five miles from the river. There are some stumps where the old warehouse used to be. Captain Anderson states that once when the river was on a big rise he unloaded lumber from the *Flour Bluff* right there in the back door of Borden's store. The river must have been about five miles wide, extending northward right over to White's Point. From Borden's back door Captain Anderson went all the way to Meansville, which was west of White's Point on the north shore of

---

[40] The Whites included the families of brothers Edward and Frank White, many of whom died in the yellow fever epidemic of 1867. White's Point became known as White Point, the site of D. C. Rachal's ranch house.

Nueces Bay, and customarily not reached by boat. There was no bridge across the river in those days. Hearn's Ferry was used to reach Meansville and Borden's Ferry to reach Sharpsburg.

When it was proposed to build the Aransas Pass railroad across the Nueces Bay, approximately at White's Point, Captain Anderson used the *Flour Bluff* to make the soundings and survey. He found there was such a depth of mud that the crossings had to be located on the reef — the present crossing.

During the 1870s the business and occupations of the communities were centered very much on the ox-cart trains used to bring hides and wool from Mexico. Even oranges and lemons and Mexican sugar known as piloncillo were imported in this manner. There was no sugar cane grown in Texas at this time. During these early days the merchants in Corpus Christi were J. B. Mitchell, George Evans, Headen & Sons, and Shier. Mr. Shier[41] was murdered for refusing to extend credit to a disreputable character who had a reputation for having killed several people. A man by the name of John Fogg, who owned a livery stable, and who was chief of the Fire Department, got a mob together and went out to hang this man, Jim Garner.[42] They hung him out from town in an arroyo with about a hundred yards of rope.

At that time the City Market (Plate 25) was where the City Hall is now.[43] It was built and conducted on the order of the Mexican markets and opened at 3 a.m. Anderson said that during that time you could get a basket full of meat for a quarter but now you have to have a basket full of money to get a quarter of a pound of meat.

The Morgan and Mallory steamers came into the bay as early as 1875. The Morgan liner *Mary* was deeply loaded when she struck the bar, the water being too shallow on the bar for her to make the crossing. There were about 25 passengers on board. She was carrying 7,000 barrels of freight (the various boxes, sacks, etc., of freight were all weighed and the total weight stated as barrels),

---

[41] Emanuel Scheur opened a store in the Staples Building on Chaparral.

[42] Scheuer and Garner apparently knew each other. They served together in W. S. Shaw's Confederate militia company. Muster rolls list Scheur as a corporal and Garner a private.

[43] On Market Square, between Peoples and Schatzell on Mesquite Street.

which were all lost. It was scattered from Port Aransas to Point Isabel, all along Padre Beach, and there was flour lying along the beach for miles.

The steamers coming to Corpus Christi would come right up to Central Wharf (Plate 15). Before the steamers came, schooners would bring freight to Rockport, as there was no channel to Corpus then. Captain Heath[44] came here from Rio de Janeiro with a load of coffee, and he went down to lighter the steamer, the *Martha M. Heath.* The first time he came to Corpus Christi he came up with me. On the way back he said, "I like the looks of this country; I think I'll locate here." He went to Rockport, to Port Aransas and looked around. He came to Corpus Christi and said, "You ought to get a company to build a wharf at Port Aransas about three miles from where the Lighthouse is now." They raised the company in Corpus Christi and built the wharf, and the steamers landed there instead of at Rockport. This killed Rockport, and they felt like killing Captain Heath. This must have been about 1878 or '79.

Captain Fly used to have a cotton gin right near the shore. Two brothers and a brother-in-law came from New York with him and located here.

The ranchers would take wool and hides to Aransas. Sometimes there would be two or three thousand hides piled up on the schooner at one time. The wool dealers were John Woessner (Plate 12), Norwick Gussett, Edey & Kirsten (Plate 9) and Ed Buckley, who succeeded Edey & Kirsten, who were located opposite the old St. James Hotel.

For the benefit of the Mexicans who brought the wool, the various dealers had distinctive wind vanes on top of their buildings. Mr. Gussett had a rooster and to the Mexicans this was the place of the "*gallo.*" Mr. Woessner had a horse on his warehouse, and his place was known as "*el caballo.*" Kirsten had a sheep on his building and consequently a Mexican who was to go to Kirsten's place merely had to be told to go to the "*borrego.*" These vanes were made of tin or zinc.

---

[44] Captain Cheston C. Heath later built a store on Market Square and was elected mayor. His son was president of the school board.

Mr. DeRyee had a little shop this side (west) of the present location of the Nueces Hotel.[45] He made candles and fishing lines. A candle mold consists of little tubes in a row — three, four or five — about as long as the candle was to be. Twine was placed in the centers of the tubes and the melted tallow poured in. Tallow candles furnished the only means of lighting during the Civil War.

Mr. J. M. Moore was dredging a canal to Corpus Christi and Captain Anderson's father worked on this dredge. "After this dredge was abandoned on account of the Civil War coming on, it gradually went to pieces. The city built another dredge to make the Morris and Cummings channel so the steamers could come in. It was to be paid for with sections of land for each portion of the channel built. They sent two young fellows down here, 25 or so years old. One was named McSpirit. The dredge was nearly a wreck so they went to work with a lot of men and in a month they had it in working shape again. It was a dipper dredge and it worked night and day." Captain Anderson furnished them wood bought from Mr. Rachal at White's Point. This may have been about 1870.

During the last of the 1870s and first of the 1880s, Corpus Christi and the surrounding country were undergoing much development, as can be imagined by the lumber schooners arriving here. The lumber came from Calcasieu, La. The schooners belonged to Mr. Daniel Goss, who was said to have had 13 daughters and one son. Four or five of these were acquaintances of Captain Anderson. One of the daughters married a Mr. F. G. Moeling, who operated a lumber yard in Corpus Christi. A Mr. W. E. Richards married one of the daughters and was associated with Sidney Borden up the river at Sharpsburg.

"Mr. Richards lived on Padre. His sisters visited here from Calcasieu. I took them down in the boat. They were all pretty. On New Year's Eve we sat the old year out and the New Year in, playing smut. We were all as black as any Negroes ever made. We had coffee, cakes and everything — a couple of turkeys, etc. — all on a round table. The girls stayed there about a week and enjoyed

---

[45] On the northwest corner at Peoples and Chaparral, where the City National Bank was later built.

going up and down the beach gathering shells." George Locke married another daughter.

These lumber schooners were named *Daniel Goss*, a three-master, *Inez Houston*, and *Laurel*. The *Laurel* was lost in the storm of 1880[46] on Padre Island right at the big hill just south of Corpus Christi Pass. Another boat, the *Welcome*, may not have belonged to Goss. Six of these lumber schooners had unloaded and left Corpus Christi just before the storm of 1880 and they were all close to Galveston when they ran into the hurricane. They all ran before the hurricane and all were lost except one, the *Inez Houston*, which got into Pass Cavallo.

On the *Welcome* there were seven men all of whom were lost. During the storm she floated with her bottom up by the old Dad Grant place on Mustang Island. She had just been painted and just beyond the old ranch house settled in the sand with her center sticking up. She remained that way for more than two months and in the years that passed she either settled or the sand covered her up. The other boats went ashore further down the island. They were named *Leman No. 1* and *Leman No. 2*, *Cassador*, *Carolina*, *George Peabody*, *Nonesuch*, and *Amedia*. The *F. G. Moeling* escaped destruction.

Mr. E. D. Sidbury[47] lost his boat, the *E. D. Sidbury*, which was the first gasoline-engine-operated boat in this section and which was built in Boston. Other boats operated by Sidbury were the *Andrew Borden* and *Garnock*. Of the boats that were lost, the *Laurel* had eight men on board and only two were saved. One of the survivors was named Charles Baurop; the name of the other cannot be remembered by Captain Anderson. Charles Baurop has descendants in Rockport. He was 20 miles down Padre Island when washed ashore and three times was carried back into the Gulf. The third time he was carried in on the galley table and held behind a log. From there he crawled to the sand hills and lay worn out. When

---

[46] There were two hurricanes that year, a weaker tropical storm on June 24 followed by a more violent storm on Aug. 12, which left Padre Island littered with wrecked ships.

[47] Lumber dealer in Corpus Christi.

he awakened he found he had no clothes on and on one in sight. He walked from Murdock Hill to the head of the Island, some 20 miles, to where Pete Benson, the quarantine officer, lived. This is at Corpus Pass. When he arrived close to the house he shouted to Pete Benson and told him he had no clothes on and Pete said to come on in, that there was no one there but him. In about 20 minutes the second survivor came in.

The old Quarantine Station was a very good house on the point of the Island. It was called the Yankee House because a lot of Yankees came from Boston and went into the cattle business. They knew nothing about cattle and so finally went broke and left the house, which was sold to a fish-packing concern. Mr. Kearney was head of the fish-packing business. He was a big fat fellow. Something troubled his throat and he could sleep only sitting up and snored very loudly. William Anderson took Mr. Kearney on his boat from Flour Bluff to Corpus Christi and he stayed at the St. James Hotel, operated by William Biggio. Mr. Kearney snored so much that all the guests complained and Mr. Biggio diplomatically found him a room down near the bay. From Corpus, Mr. Kearney took the mail boat to Indianola. There were 15 persons on board and it was long remembered by the captain how all the 15 passengers were kept awake by Mr. Kearney.

The fish-canning plant at Corpus Christi Pass, at the head of the Island, canned fish chowder, and also a few fish were dried and shipped. This business was developed, however, after the close of the cattle-packing industry. Considerable equipment and money were invested in this fish-packing plant and some 50 or 60 people lived around the packing plant at that time. When you look at the beach and entrance to Corpus Christi now, one wonders how that many people could possibly live there.

During this era the city of Corpus Christi depended for drinking water on the rain caught in cement cisterns made of shell, lime and imported cement. At least three of such cisterns may still be found in Corpus Christi — one at the old Ricklefsen home, 1402 North Chaparral, one at Miss Katie McTierman's, on North Broadway, and one on Mann Street near North Broadway. Many people purified their cistern water by keeping a bag of charcoal under the spout leading to the cistern so the water going into the cistern would be clear and pure. Some built boxes for the purpose. The old cistern at the Anderson home was square in outline, instead of the round shape usually used. It was finally made useless by the penetration of roots from nearby trees, causing it to leak.

Shallow wells were made in the shell not far back from the shore and seepage water filtered from them. The stock was watered from these. It was also used for bathing purposes, and some of the population even drank it. The first Fire Department had box wells along the shore and at the end of all streets they had piers they could run hand-pump engines out on to get water. The first fire engine was operated by Sam Shoemaker. One night Shoemaker was sick and a substitute took his place and allowed the boiler to blow up. When the boiler blew up (some time in the 1870s) the smokestack went over the top of Market Hall (Plate 25) and fell in the street. For a week or so, while repairs were being made, the city had to do without the fire engine. The Fire Department also had a big well six or seven feet right back of the station. Before this engine they had a hand pump which used about eight men on each side holding the lever and pumping.

There still remains at old Indianola, the only sign of a town, a great many of these old concrete cisterns showing where the houses were. Across Copano Bay at Lamar and close to the beach are a few of these cisterns still left. There are also a few at Bayside, which was not far from old St. Mary's. St. Mary's was a little town, scattered all around, but in those days there was quite a business there. One of the firms recalled was a general merchandise store owned by Coffin Bros. Anderson carried them freight from Indianola.

The town of Indianola was not settled at the time of the Civil War. Lamar was only a settlement of a few adobe houses. Rockport was not yet a town, but Port Lavaca was a good-sized town. The Morgan steamship lines put Indianola on the map because they built a wharf there for their ships to land and they also built a little railroad.

Referring to the Indianola storm of 1875: "I took up the first boatload of supplies from Corpus Christi — food, clothing, etc.

Everything had been wrecked up there. Back of the town was Green Lake. Its sides were piled high with houses, boats, cattle — everything — all washed over against the bank on the south side especially. Many people were clinging to old pieces of boats and houses. One young lady, Susanna Pendleton, was hanging on an old piece of wreck when she drifted right across the bow of a boat which was moving along away up the country. She screamed as she brushed against the cable and was rescued. She later became the wife of Mike Brennan, Captain of the *Agnes*, one of the mail boats.

There were three mail boats — the *Henrietta*, with Captain Steinhardt; the *Emily*, with Captain William Moore, and the *Agnes*, with Captain Mike Brennan (no kin to Ed Brennan). They made three trips a week between Indianola and Corpus Christi. The *Henrietta* was at Steamboat Dugout in San Antonio Bay and she dragged her anchors away over into Matagorda Island. She had four or five passengers, Mrs. Green Holden, wife of the customs officer, being one. They were saved, but the boat was never gotten off and was a total loss. She was replaced on the mail route by the *Nellie Sweeney*.

Steamboat Dugout was at the entrance from San Antonio Bay to Espiritu Santo Bay. It was a small channel only about two or three hundred yards long. Espiritu empties into Matagorda Bay through a little channel. Port O'Connor is right on the extreme point where Espiritu empties into Matagorda. Indianola was about 10 miles nearer the point than Port Lavaca, and the place where all the boats anchored was known as the Bayou.

The farmers and everybody from up all the creeks all came down in their boats to Indianola bringing their chickens, turkeys, potatoes, honey, and eggs to market. Powder Horn preceded Indianola, but Indianola developed into a larger place because of its good harbor. "My father bought the blinds in Indianola for his house, as none were obtainable in Corpus Christi. The firm selling them was called Huck & Halfrench, who had a good lumber yard. In those days a house wasn't finished unless it had blinds."

Dan Sullivan, who in later years became a big banker in San Antonio, was a merchant and steamship agent at Indianola. "They told me he could write a letter with both hands, holding a pen in each. At any rate, he was certainly an energetic worker. One time when I was in Indianola with my boat, Dan was down on the wharf. He asked me if I could take a load of lumber to Corpus. I said yes, so he loaded it on. Then he said, 'Can you take a deck load of whisky?' I told him that I could, and he loaded the deck with about 80 barrels and half-barrels of whisky and wine. When we reached Corpus Christi, Emmert, the wholesaler, took off the wine and whisky. He found a barrel of wine leaking; it had lost about 15 gallons. One barrel of whisky turned out to be pure water. He sure was mad; said I had to pay for them. I told him to go see Dave Murphy, the agent. Well, finally I agreed to pay for the wine, as that loss was my responsibility. But I wouldn't pay for the whisky, as it had been loaded on the boat sealed, and the seal was unbroken when I delivered the cargo in Corpus. The whole matter was straightened out to the satisfaction of all when Dan Sullivan informed us that by mistake, a barrel he had soaking with water had been loaded on the boat along with the others containing whisky."

Captain Anderson has no recollection of any saddle makers in Corpus Christi during the Civil War, but does of the saddles made following the war. A man by the name of H. Keller made saddles and Kenedy had his own saddle man on his ranch. They used rawhide mostly and tanned leather when they could get it.

The first ice was brought from Maine in schooners in 1873; it was cut out in blocks four feet square and packed in sawdust. The first icehouse was built later by a man named Bruin. His icehouse was where the Masonic Lodge is today and he could make only 500 or 600 pounds a day. Ice was not used for the preservation of meat; there wasn't enough for that. It was used for cocktails and iced water. The only liquor in Corpus Christi to be had at that time was "hard" liquor. There was no beer. Later George Blucher and some other man built an icehouse close to E. H. Caldwell's warehouse. Blucher bought out his partner and went into business with Mr. Ward.

There is a difference of opinion about the supply of milk, butter and cheese. There was always a plentiful supply of these in Corpus Christi and the people practically lived on them, although out on the ranches the supply was scarce. Captain Andy Anderson remembers the necessity of milking eight or ten cows a day and recalls vividly that he had to churn lots of butter. This butter sold at a price of 25 to 35 cents a pound. Often he would try to sneak away from the churning and go fishing but his mother's sharp eye usually caught him before he made such an escape.

It seems as if all the children were just as fat as could be, and this is partly explained by the fact that they often helped themselves to drinks of sweet milk, fresh and warm, direct from the cow. Pasteurization was unheard of, and no one worried about diseases being carried through the milk. The young men on the boats were strong as young lions. The first thing in the morning came the hoisting of sails, which were 40 to 50 feet high, and it meant lots of good exercise. "We had plenty of food and we worked all day, and sometimes all night, and never thought anything about it."

There was an abundance of beef, mutton and goat meat. There were lots of fish and oysters and it was not an uncommon thing to go down to the bay and catch fish for breakfast. "Sometimes we would even gig the fish; I was a good gigger and could gig a mullet almost as far away as I could see it."

One of the first exports from Corpus Christi after the arrival of the railroad was turtles, many of these weighing 200 pounds or more. Some shipments were even made by boat, the turtles going out over the Morgan Line, with their flippers tied, but the turtles still alive. The turtles were usually caught in seines. John Superach[48] was the leading fish man in Corpus Christi then. He built a pen out in the water, making a fence of piling to keep turtles in and fed them on mullets. There were a few loggerhead turtles — they had big heads. When an order for turtles came in, and a boat was ready to take them away, Superach had only to go to his pen, get the wanted ones and weigh them.

Sometimes the turtles would come up on land. "One time over on Mustang Island one came up near where I was living. Its tracks, about six feet wide, where his flippers scraped the sand, were seen by my wife and another woman, Nevada Steen, as they came down

---

[48] John Superach, pioneer fish and oyster dealer, died at his home on Water Street on Nov. 4, 1892.

the beach on horseback. It was night before we started off with a wagon and lantern to hunt the turtle. We followed the tracks, and although we did not find the turtle, we dug around in the sand until we uncovered a nest with about 150 eggs. Turtle eggs are similar to pullet eggs, but the shells are soft; you can squeeze one of them and the dent will stay in for a long time. They taste something like gull eggs, and are very good eating. Turtle meat was usually prepared in soup, which tasted much better than when fried."

"Nevada Steen had lived in Florida and she said that there the turtles were sometimes seven feet wide. If one of these big fellows came lumbering along over the sand as she was on her way to go fishing, she would jump on its back and ride to the beach." In 1886, a big freeze killed them out so that you rarely see any now except a straggler in the Gulf.

There was a big lighthouse that stood on the hill in front of Gussett's residence. It was built by the U.S. government between 1851 and 1852; after the Civil War the Confederates had their arsenal there and stored their gunpowder in it. It had quite a ditch dug around it. The Confederates blew it up to keep it from falling into the hands of the Yankees.

To think of what happened in those days; a number of boys, including Captain Andy Anderson, crawled through a window into the lighthouse about 12 feet from the ground and into a room where the gunpowder was stored. They filled an old wooden churn with gunpowder and took it out. As matches were scarce in those days, one of the boys, Frank Hooper, went home for a firebrand. By the time he returned the others had laid out a path of powder some distance from the churn. At first it was difficult to ignite but suddenly it blew up, making a smoke and fire like the blowing out of walls in this vicinity. The boys took to their heels and the constable after them. They first hid in the old cemetery, but decided they weren't far enough away, so slipped out to the old Salt Lake. From there they could see the smoke rising and they thought the powder would never stop burning. When the darkness fell they all went home, and so far as is known, no one ever discovered who the culprits were. Only one casualty was listed. One of the boys was hit in the back by the bottom of the churn as he was beating a retreat.

Captain Andy Anderson recalls that during the 1870s the boys made much of what has always been known as the Salt Lake. This was quite a lake and very pretty. They used to go out there and shoot ducks in the evening. At that time the water was four or five feet deep and the shores were beautiful with green shrubs growing right down to the water's edge. Frequently cattle waded out in the lake and bogged down in the mud, particularly when the water was very low. Sometimes when they would bog down they would drown and a number of people made considerable profit putting ropes on their horns and dragging the animals out for their hides.

Captain John Anderson's sympathies were aroused in behalf of the poor cattle during these droughts and from his own pocket he paid the expense of having some Mexicans dig long trenches along the shell near the beach, close to the Anderson home, into which would seep fresh water. The cattle could smell the water a long way off and would come down to drink. The men often watched the wild-eyed and thirsty ones come to the water; they would pay no attention to their surroundings but when satisfied would look around and race away.

The first yellow fever that Captain Anderson recalls was brought in by a man from Indianola who was staying here in a hotel in 1867.[49] When yellow fever struck New Orleans, a steamer, the *Arkansas*, carrying freight from New Orleans to Corpus Christi, was stopped at Aransas Pass by the quarantine customs and was refused admittance. The steamer negotiated a trade with a bunch of lighter schooners to take off the freight, and lay in quarantine the required 28 days. Captain Anderson owned one of these boats. They went up to St. Joseph's Island and anchored side by side. Each boat had its own musicians and for a time they were very gay. Dr. Burks was the quarantine officer and he told them to hoist an American flag if anybody took sick. A man by the name of Henry Rogers came down with chills and fever, they hoisted the flag and

---

[49] J.S. Snyder from Washington, D.C. rode in on horseback from Indianola, where an outbreak of yellow fever was raging, and got a room at Ziegler's Hotel. He soon died of the fever.

the quarantine doctor was sent for. The crews were very quiet and worried until they were told it was malaria.

"During these days we frolicked in the water a great deal of the time. I was a good swimmer and feared no one in the water. One day I was sitting at the edge of a boat when a Greek, Frank Ford, Captain of the *Emma Clara,* came along and threatened to push me over. He scuffled a while and then we both tumbled into the water. Poor Frank Ford couldn't swim much and I made it harder for him by pushing his head under every time he came up gasping for breath. Finally he hollered he'd had enough, and I let him alone. As he pulled himself up one of the many ropes we had hanging from the boat's sides, I swam under the boat, which drew about five feet, came up on the opposite side, and enjoyed the scene as the Greek called out an alarm that I had drowned, as he couldn't see me anymore. I swam back of the boat and climbed up on the rudder, still hidden from sight from above. Some got out long hooks with which they scraped for my body. When he finally spied me sitting calmly on the rudder he was as mad as a man could be."

"On about the 18th day the doctor said we might go ashore, so several went to Paul's Ranch, opposite Rockport, and got two sheep. They skinned them, and we had plenty of mutton after that. About the 20th day some of the boys went down to Aransas Pass in the little sailboats. The next day pilots Ed and John Mercer returned the call. As they came up in their yawls some of the fellows planned a surprise for the visitors, as a sort of initiation to the bunch. Buckets of water were placed inside the ship railing where they were unseen from below. As the small boats came alongside, the Mercers received a good drenching. But they took it all right and didn't get mad."

After 21 days had elapsed the doctor came out and fumigated each vessel's hold. They were told they could go up to Shell Bank and stay the remainder of the time. (After crossing Corpus Christi Bay and then going for about six miles through the Morris and Cummings Cut, Shell Bank is on the left as you come out of the channel.)

When they got back to Corpus Christi they were met by a shotgun mob and were refused admittance. While the schooners were being held off in the dark the crews quietly disembarked in their light boats and were downtown having milk shakes while the crowd held the larger vessels off. The names of these vessels were *Flour Bluff* (Plate 8), *Alice, Emma Clara, Rest Ripple, St. Joe,* and *Two Brothers.* The next day the City Council met to decide what was to be done with the perishable part of the freight — fruit, potatoes, onions, etc. It was decided to load it on the *Leona* and have it taken to Portland and dumped. The *Leona* was a three-masted schooner owned by Norwick Gussett.

It was after the Civil War before the yellow fever epidemic broke out in Corpus Christi. There were then a thousand inhabitants and over 300[50] of them died of the fever. Many tried to escape the plague by going to White's Point or Banquete, but fell victims to it anyway. Little was known of the origin and cause of yellow fever then, and had they gone in the other direction toward the bluff or to Padre Island, and escaped the mosquitoes they would not have died. "It was awful. People nearly went crazy. There were no doctors[51] and hardly any nurses. On the street nobody could be seen, unless an occasional person running across. Smoke from tar buckets filled with burning charcoal hung over the streets. This was used to fumigate against the fever."

Dr. Merriman's treatment was to fill a tub with hot ashes and hot water and make the patient plunge his feet and legs into it. The patient was swathed in blankets and made to sweat the fever out of his system. The pest house, located somewhere near where Antelope Street crosses North Carancahua, belonged to Dan Johnson, a Negro. One of the men on Captain John Anderson's boat contracted the fever and was taken to this house. Captain Andy Anderson later carried his clothes to him. "When I reached him where he lay on the floor in the center of the room, he yelled, 'You little fool! What are you doing here? Can't you see all these people have died of the yellow fever?' He was referring to seven or eight

---

[50] Joseph Almond kept a tally in his diary of each day's death during the yellow fever epidemic. His record showed that 135 people died of the fever.

[51] After the town's three doctors died during the epidemic.

52

corpses in the room. 'Well,' I said, 'we have it at home, so what difference does it make?' The man recovered."

When the jetty was built at Aransas Pass about 1880, Captain John Anderson had the contract to carry the rocks from Laguna Madre and carried the first load of rock for the jetty. This was taken out of Laguna Madre in Baffin Bay, from the location near Peñascal, known to us today as the Point of Rocks. It is a peculiar limestone formation which can be seen at low tide. Up to the time of the 1919 storm he had brought in the old *Flour Bluff* (Plate 8) a quantity of this rock formation, and out of this was built a special breakwater in front of the old Seaside Hotel. It was also used along a number of the water lots of the present Water Street.

Returning to the building of the jetty, Captain John Anderson had approximately 100 men and 15 schooners engaged in digging rock out of the Laguna Madre and carrying it to the jetty in front of what is now Port Aransas. In order to load the schooners, which were in deep water, Captain Anderson had flatboats on which the rock was loaded, and by means of a pulley and cable it was pulled to the schooner. These schooners carried about 25 tons of rock at a time. The amount of rock on the contract was measured by calculating three cubic feet to a ton.

To place the rock in the proper position for the jetty, special brush mattresses were woven and tied together. Only a few people have ever seen this work done. The brush used for this purpose was sweet bay, which grew along the shore near Rockport. When this was used up, then live oak brush was brought in. There was an important contract for bringing this brush from Rockport. It was put in bundles small enough to carry under the arm, men being paid 10 cents a bundle.

In preparation for the making of the mattresses, they stuck sticks in the ground close together. The brush was laid between these sticks until enough was accumulated; then one of the men would come along with a tarred rope and tie the brush tightly together, making a row perhaps 75 feet long. They would make a short row about 25 feet long and then a long one, alternating rows in length. These rows were laid upon a platform which was built on an incline; the brush ropes were held in place by sticks to keep them from slipping off. They were laid crisscross, the long ropes lengthwise and the short ones crosswise, with small spaces in between, through which they were tied together with heavier rope or marlin. They were about five feet thick when finished. When this was completed, a tug would come alongside the platform and the mattresses were tied onto the tug and towed into the bay where they would throw rocks on the mattresses. This would sink the mattresses into the water, making a solid foundation for the remainder of the rocks.

When the government tore up these old jetties in 1889 or 1890, they took up some of these old mattresses. The wood was found to still be green and showed no indication of rotting, due no doubt to having been completely submerged in saltwater.

At the time this work was done, the lighthouse on St. Joseph's Island was opposite the bar or entrance to the pass. Since then the jetties have caused shoaling on the St. Joseph side of the pass and cut away on the sand on the Mustang Island side until at present the old lighthouse is a mile or more north of the entrance to the pass. Colonel Mansfield was the engineer in charge of building the Mansfield Jetty and the method used was the same as used at Port Eads at the mouth of the Mississippi.

At present there is only a small cove where the boats land at the little town of Port Aransas. When the government had troops in camp there during the war (2,000 or 3,000 soldiers), it was a large cove. At the time the building of the jetty was going on, the Andersons had a shipyard on Mustang Island, headquarters for their work. "In 1880, while I was living down there, the big storm of that year cut a deep channel right through the island. It remained open about a month, and then it filled up at the east end, the Gulf side, but remained deep on the inside. One day I threw my cast-net into this part of it and drew up a catch of two dozen sharks about 14 inches long. Had they come in from the Gulf? Maybe so, or maybe they had been born there. You hear a lot about the danger of sharks, but sharks are not so bad."

The other items of interest regarding the old-timers, contributed by Captain Anderson are: The Curry family came to the Island after the Civil War and settled on Padre Island below Pat Dunn's Ranch. The ranch, four miles below Shamrock Cove, was owned by Jonas Grant, who had about 1,500 head of sheep on the island. Anderson lived there awhile.

Andrew Anderson (1852-1949) (Plate 5) arrived in Corpus Christi in 1852 with his parents, Mr. and Mrs. John Anderson, when he was a year old. He became a sea captain and shipbuilder and bay pilot like his father before him. He worked for Mifflin Kenedy for many years, hauling fence lumber and supplies for his Laureles and later La Parra ranches. He met Mary Grant at the Port Aransas Lighthouse and they married in 1890. She died in 1915. He was the owner of the pleasure boat *Japonica* and was nearly drowned when his ship *Gipsy* was wrecked ashore in the 1919 storm. Information for his reminiscences was collected by E. L. Caldwell from talks with Capt. Anderson in Corpus Christi in 1940. Captain Andrew Anderson died Oct. 9, 1949, three years short of his 100th birthday.

CHAPTER 4

ANNA MOORE SCHWIEN RECOLLECTIONS

My mother, Malvina Britton, more than 90 years old at the time of her death in 1910, was of Negro and Indian blood. She was one of the earliest slaves in Corpus Christi, arriving here on Jan. 1, 1849 with the Baskin family from Mississippi. When the Corpus Christi business partnership of John Baskin, William Mann and Forbes Britton was dissolved, mother was left to Capt. Britton.

Some time in the 1850s Capt. Britton and Mr. George Wilkins Kendall, who had drawn a white bean at the castle of Perote,[1] were partners in the sheep business and my mother was placed by Capt. Britton on Mr. Kendall's sheep ranch near New Braunfels. Here I was born May 15, 1856. Mrs. Georgina Kendall Fellowes, daughter of Mr. Kendall, verifies this date, as it was just after the Kendalls arrived at the ranch. My mother returned to the Brittons in Corpus Christi when I was five months old.

During the 1850s and early 1860s she spent much time on various ranches, as well as at Fort Merrill, where she was placed by Capt. Britton for a while with Capt. Samuel Plummer's family. There she spent several years, always recalled as years of lonesomeness because the fort was isolated and there were no friends to visit. Capt. Plummer, who had been stationed in Corpus

---

[1] The drawing of the beans was at Rancho Salado, not Perote.

Christi following the Mexican War, is buried in the military cemetery on Government Hill in San Antonio.

In 1863 we went to the Evans ranch, about 28 miles from Corpus Christi. It was known as the Barranco Blanco[2] ranch, which means white hillside. In 1865 we came back to Corpus Christi to live. I was nine years old then.

My father was Sam Moore, a slave on the plantation of Col. John M. Moore in Alabama. Col. Moore had many slaves, and to keep them occupied and make use of their time, he established different industries, such as a foundry, marble works, etc. Papa worked in the foundry as a puddler. Papa left Alabama following a fight with a white man and came to Texas. During the next four years he made many trips into Mexico, where he could have lived as a free man if he had desired, but he preferred the States. When the Moores came to Corpus Christi, Papa again joined Col. Moore as a slave. On one occasion, Col. Moore took him to Mexico with him on a trip. While there, the colonel said to him, "Sam, you know you are free down here in Mexico. I can't require you to return to the States with me." Papa told him that if he had wanted his freedom he had had many opportunities to run away before the Moores came to Texas. He remained a faithful slave until freedom came as a result of the war.

My mother's recollection of the early days in Corpus Christi was very vivid and she related many a time the story of the coming of the Baskin family to this little settlement. John Baskin's sister, Esther, was already here, the wife of William Mann, and it was for the purpose of visiting the Manns that the Baskins left their Mississippi home in 1848, hoping to arrive here by Christmas. Their departure had been delayed on account of disturbed conditions following the Mexican War, and further delays occurred at New Orleans and Galveston. At the latter place they had expected the boat, the *Swan*, to meet them, but its non-arrival for two weeks prevented the Christmas reunion they had anticipated.

---

[2] Barranco Blanco was one of Henry Kinney's four ranch properties sold for debt; the others were the Rincón del Oso, El Alazán and Mustang Island.

They finally reached Corpus Christi on the first day of the new year of 1849.

There was a close bond of friendship between the three families of Baskin, Mann and Britton. John Baskin, William Mann, and Forbes Britton were business partners in Corpus Christi for many years. In addition, Mr. Mann was Mr. Baskin's brother-in-law. Another brother-in-law was John Redmond, who married Miss Louisa Baskin. The sisters, Miss Eliza and Miss Laura Baskin, did not marry.

Capt. Forbes Britton, an army officer, had been down here during the Mexican War and had mustered out about 1848. Mrs. Britton before her marriage was Miss Rebecca Millard, of an old Baltimore family that had become wealthy through land grants. She had a brother, Dr. Millard, living in Grand Cateur, La., and two sisters, Mrs. Persifor Smith, and Mrs. Josiah Armstrong, at Fort Gibson, Ark.[3] While visiting these sisters, she met and married Forbes Britton in 1836, and they soon returned to Baltimore. It was shortly after his Mexican service that he brought the family to Corpus Christi, where he met Mr. Baskin and Mr. Mann and went into business with them.

My mother told me that when she arrived with the Baskins on Jan. 1, 1849, Capt. Britton's house on the bluff was being built, having been started the previous year (Plate 13). She also said that below the Britton house you could see pits in the cliffs where they dug out clay for making bricks to build Mr. Mann's red house on the beach. The builders of the Britton house were Berry, Gravis[4] and Yates, and Pedro Hinojosa was one of the workmen. The front of the house is just exactly as it was built, but the roof has been changed. The ell, too, is different, as originally it was two-story. This building, at 411 North Broadway, is still standing in its original location.

---

[3] Fort Gibson was in Indian Territory, near the Arkansas River, in today's eastern Oklahoma.

[4] Henry W. Berry and J.A.F. Gravis were the builders of many of the early shellcrete structures in Corpus Christi, including the Britton house, which is known as Centennial House today.

The firm of Britton, Mann and Baskin operated a freight line between Galveston and Corpus Christi, shipping out finely cured hides and skins from Mexico. It would sometimes take three weeks to make the trip from Galveston to Corpus Christi because of the shallow water across the bar, and for this reason they required three boats to maintain the service. One of these was the packet, *Swan*, and I think another was called the *Constitution*. When the business partnership was discontinued, each partner received one of the boats, the *Swan* going to Capt. Britton.

Capt. Britton had acquired a ranch at the Oso, about eight miles in the country, referred to as Britton Motts. Here, some time probably in the 1850s, they built a ranch house, using in it part of the old sailboat *Swan*. This ranch house at the Oso had a long wide front gallery, which is so much like the gallery on the house where Mrs. Ed Cubage is living (415 North Tancahua) that I am reminded of it every time I pass this place. The gallery at the ranch, however, was even longer and was very wide.[5]

The Brittons had two daughters and a son. A great deal of entertaining was done, both at the Corpus Christi home and at the ranch. The women in those days dressed *so* well. The materials were of the finest, and the dresses fitted well. Not a day passed that the women didn't dress in the afternoon after their naps. Dressing was carefully done, and was followed by sewing or other pleasant pastimes.

One of the daughters, Anne Elizabeth, and the only son, Edward, were twins, and the other daughter was Rebecca. The son, a surgeon in the Confederate Army, married Miss Bessie Ware; he died in 1865 and is buried in Holy Cross Cemetery in Corpus Christi. His widow was later a governess in the home of Mrs. Henrietta King.

Miss Elizabeth, known as "Lizzie" to her friends, married E. J. Davis, a young lawyer in Corpus Christi, in 1858. Both before and after her marriage she was an excellent musician, playing the harp, guitar, organ and piano. Her mother, also a musician, played the old

---

[5] The Britton ranch house, which Mrs. Britton called "Tres Ninos" for her three children, was on the Cayo del Oso, five miles southwest of Corpus Christi.

melodeon in the first Catholic church here. Mr. Davis became a district judge and was away from home a great deal. His wife remained at the Britton ranch, where two children were born; the first child died. A third was born later at the home in Corpus Christi.

Rebecca Britton married Charles Worthington, probably in 1861 or 1862. I remember the wedding well, as it took place at the ranch at the Oso. The Worthingtons were wealthy and many relatives came to attend; many elegant presents were received. Music was made by two Mexican musicians, a violinist and a guitarist, and Theodore Lawrence, son of Dr. D. H. Lawrence, who played the violin well.

Capt. Forbes Britton, besides having been in the sheep and cattle ranching business, also engaged in politics, serving as senator in the Texas Legislature. My mother told me that his last public speech was made at the corner of Chaparral and William streets, against Secession, as he was a Unionist. He died in Austin.[6] The coffin was lined inside with satin and had on top, outside, a silver plate with his name. Capt. Britton was a High Church man; his wife was a Catholic. He had family connections with prominent people in New Orleans, especially those who owned the *New Orleans Picayune*.

After her husband's death, Mrs. Britton moved from the ranch to town. I think this was probably in 1862 — I know it was cold weather. She made her home in the Redmond cottage on the bluff, in the same yard with the Mann home, living alone, as her two daughters were away. The Worthingtons had left this country because of the war, as they didn't want to take up arms; and the Davises had left because of Mr. Davis's strong Northern sympathies.

E. J. Davis was a Unionist and favored abolishing slavery. He opposed Secession. Why they disliked him so I don't know, just because he was for the Union. He took active part in the federal

---

[6] Forbes Britton was sick when he went to Austin for a special session of the Legislature in February 1861. He died of pneumonia on Feb. 14, 1861. He was the third man buried in the State Cemetery in Austin.

cause, and one time organized a company of federal troops in this vicinity. Cesario Falcón was captain and many of the members were old Mexicans who had fought in the war for Texas independence. Others included Larry, Joe and Matt Dunn.

Some time in 1863, I think it was, Mr. Davis was captured by the Confederates and taken to Brownsville, where they planned to hang him.[7] One of leading military men of Mexico heard about it and sent word at once to Brownsville that if they carried out their plans he would burn the entire city. Davis was writing what he thought would be his last letter to his wife, when someone came for him and put him on a gunboat which went to Corpus Christi, where his wife and two children met it at the old Mann wharf, and were taken aboard and away, for safety. Gen. Lew Wallace, author of "Ben Hur," was said to have been on board that vessel.

After the war, Miss Lizzie and her husband returned to Corpus Christi, where they built a fine home on the bluff. They were popular with a large circle of friends, and their home was a center of society. Mr. Davis became governor of Texas in 1869, and after this time they never came back to Corpus Christi to live. He died in the early 1880s and was buried in Austin. I had a letter from Mrs. Davis not long after his death, saying that she was living in Grand Cateur with her uncle, Dr. Millard, and her aunt, so as to be as near as possible to her husband's last resting place.[8]

A year or so later, I was on the stage going to San Patricio to teach. You took the stagecoach to Twelve Mile Motts, then took the ferry across the river, then took the stage again. One of the other passengers was Bishop Manucy, the first bishop to come to Corpus Christi after the Civil War. He did not come from Montgomery, Ala., as was stated in an article in the paper, but came directly from Baltimore, Md. I said to him that I understood he was from Baltimore and asked if he knew the Millards, who were a prominent family there. He knew them very well, he said. When I asked if he

---

[7] Davis and his aide, Capt. W. W. Montgomery, were captured by Confederates on the Mexican side and taken across the river. Montgomery was hanged and Davis came close to being hanged before he was freed.

[8] We assume she means rather than living near other Millard relatives in Baltimore.

knew Mrs. Davis, a granddaughter of the Millards, imagine my amazement when he told me she wasn't Mrs. Davis any longer, but Mrs. "Pots" Smith. When I expressed my surprise that she had married again so soon, the bishop explained that Mr. Smith had courted Miss "Lizzie" Britton before she had become Mrs. Davis. Mr. Smith's nickname was due to his being in the pot-making business.

Her two sons, Britton and Walter Davis, are probably still living. The former was last heard from in California, and the latter in El Paso, Texas.

Mrs. Forbes Britton, whose maiden name was Millard, had two sisters who married brothers. Anne Monica married Frank W. Armstrong; and later, Gen. Persifor Smith. Another sister married Josiah Armstrong. The latter with his wife came to Corpus Christi toward the end of the Civil War and stayed at the Britton home. Due to too much drink, he was a rather rough character and was not well-liked generally. One evening he didn't return to the house for supper. After waiting for him for a while, they began a search, and found his dead body on the other side of the Salt Lake. He was buried in the burial plot in the garden of the Mann home.

Mrs. Frank Armstrong's son, Frank C., came here after the war. He had been a general in the Confederate Army, during which time he had acquired the title of "the wizard of the saddle."[9] He died of consumption.

The Brittons were great friends of the Moore family during the early days. Col. John M. Moore, a man of great wealth, brought his family here from Alabama, where he owned, among other interests, extensive iron works. He undertook the opening of a canal between Corpus Christi and Aransas Pass (channel). He owned his dredge boat, which was manned by Capt. Riddle.[10] Several other white men and many of Moore's Negroes were engaged in work on the dredge. Although the project was not a success, being uncompleted on account of the coming on of the war, the dredge boat did reach

---

[9] Brig. Gen. Frank Armstrong commanded a brigade in Gen. Braxton Bragg's Army of the Mississippi.

[10] Capt. J. C. Riddle.

Corpus Christi. When work was stopped, the boat was docked at the wharf alongside the Ritter Pavilion, where it could be seen for many, many years, but gradually disappeared as people went there and cut it up for firewood.

During the war many of the wealthy people fled Corpus Christi to Goliad, among these being the Moores. They had perfectly beautiful silver and fine chinaware, linens and carpet. Some of their belongings they started off to Goliad by wagon. But they shipped their rugs, furniture and many smaller things by wagon to a river — probably the San Antonio — which was deep enough for boats to come up, where they were loaded on a schooner to be sent to Goliad. The family went by carriage. The wagon load of goods reached its destination safely, but the water shipment failed to arrive. After waiting a reasonable time, Col. Moore made an investigation. It was found that the boat had run on a ridge in the river and everything aboard had been lost.

Col. Moore was interested in geology as well as canal dredging. He was one of the first to bore for oil in the state of Texas, his operations being at Spindletop. It seems that after Col. Moore's death someone wanting to bore near this location found some old machinery there that belonged to him. Mr. George Conklin, Col. Moore's son-in-law, told Mr. George Evans, another son-in-law, about it, and Mr. Evans was instrumental many years later in selling the machinery for $150.

Col. and Mrs. Moore's home was in the north part of town at the edge of the bay, about where Fitzgerald Street is, although at that time the water did not come so close in to Water Street as it does now; there was a curve in the shore so that the house was about a block west of the present shoreline. The home was a center of hospitality, with the four daughters receiving much attention from the young men of the town. Mary Ann, the oldest daughter, married first, Charles Jones, a lawyer, and after his death, a Mr. Sinclair. Margaret Louise married Mr. William Headen. Cornelia married George Evans, whose ranch home was near Banquete. And Hannah became Mrs. George Conklin.

A sister of George Evans married J. B. Mitchell, whose initials, J. B., stood for John Belden. The middle name was his mother's maiden name, for Sarah Belden had married William Mitchell, the first Presbyterian preacher here. I have in my trunk the chemise that Sarah Belden made for her trousseau; it is of pure linen and is entirely made by hand with the finest of stitches. Mr. J. B. Mitchell was their only son.

Mr. and Mrs. J. B. Mitchell had nine children, but only three lived beyond childhood, Edgar, Mortimer, and Rachel.

Mrs. Sarah Belden's brother, Frederick Belden, was very wealthy and also very prominent in early affairs in Corpus Christi. Belden Street was named in his memory. The father of Sarah and Frederick Belden had helped build the Erie Canal, and it was said that Sarah was the first woman to ride on the Erie Canal.

When Col. Moore came to Texas, he had with him Dr. William DeRyee, a chemist and geologist, who helped in the making of soap and candles and such things, which were used by the men on the colonel's dredge boat. Later on, Dr. DeRyee owned a drugstore here for many years, and after retiring from this business he lived in Mexico.

There were many fine people here in early days. Gen. Barney Bee had brought his family to Texas from Virginia. The Bees had so many Negroes they didn't know where they all were; they were scattered all around, from Seguin down to Corpus. The Bees were so good to them, too. I knew one of them, old Aunt Sally, well. When a widower, Gen. Bee courted Miss Lizzie Britton, unsuccessfully. His son, Hamilton P. Bee, known as "Hamp," made this his home for quite a while, living where the telephone building is now.

Capt. John Dix, living near the edge of the bay, was an importer, not a pirate as some asserted. He owned his own ships and would make distant trips to bring in such things as olive oil for sale here. His title of captain came from being a ship captain and not from being an army officer. His wife, who was Mary Eliza Hayes before she married, taught school at her home here, colored girls in the morning and white girls in the afternoon. The Dixes had two daughters, Fannie, who did not marry, and Mary, who married a Mr. Russell. A son John was a surveyor and was known as John J., to distinguish him from his father. Mr. Russell built a home for his wife at the corner of Chaparral and Taylor, probably in the late 1840s or early 1850s; this is where Mrs. Royal Givens lives now.[11]

Mrs. Helen B. Chapman, wife of Major Chapman, was a very beautiful woman from North Carolina. She was the mother of W.B. Chapman, who married Miss Jessie Rankin, and grandmother of William Warren, Nellie and Jessie Chapman.

Some of the early residents had come to Corpus Christi at the time of the Mexican War. Capt. Forbes Britton headed a company of Irishmen, of which Cornelius Cahill was sutler (a position something like a druggist)[12] and Joseph E. FitzSimmons was company clerk. These and many others were mustered out in Corpus Christi and remained as citizens or later returned with their families.

General Harney was a tall old gentleman who had seen service in the Mexican War, coming here after the war was over. He wore the *nicest* clothes; his cuffs were turned back over his coat sleeves; his collar was always so neat. He owned a great deal of land here.[13]

Judge James Webb, who lived a few miles from town,[14] had three sons, Tom, Charles and James. The Mary B. Hubbard who married Col. Kinney was said to be a daughter of the Webbs, but my mother told me she was not, that she was a niece whom the Webbs had reared. Her first husband's name was usually called "Herbert," but it was "Hubbard," my mother said.

Judge M. P. Norton and family also lived out near the Webbs, and were their close friends. Mr. C. G. Norton, who has written a story of the life of Col. Kinney, is a grandson of Judge Norton.

---

[11] Eli Merriman recalled this house, known as the Russell place, then the Ironclad Oath house, then the Royal Givens home, was built several years earlier and had served as a commissary building for Zachary Taylor's army in 1845. It was located at 802 Chaparral.

[12] A sutler was a storekeeper authorized and commissioned by the Army to sell goods on a military post.

[13] Gen. William S. Harney was famous for being the officer in charge of hanging U. S. Army deserters who were part of the San Patricio Battalion that fought in the Mexican Army. He owned the Harney Tract, which included much of the Ocean Drive land today.

[14] James Webb served as secretary of Treasury, secretary of state, and attorney general of the Republic of Texas. He had a large farm at Avery Point.

Somers Kinney, a brother or other close relative[15] of Col. Kinney, ran the *Ranchero*, a newspaper here. He was a big man, very erect, and always wore black clothes and a linen duster. He would hang the duster on the gallery when he went to court Miss Josephine Cooper, whom he married. I don't remember the date, but her father's home was at the corner of Mann and Tiger streets. Warren Kinney was here, too. I always thought of him as a brother of Somers Kinney and the Colonel, but I'm not sure just how they were related.[16] Col. Kinney was a popular man but not handsome; in fact, he was a very ordinary looking person. He died in 1865, I'm sure, even though others do say it was in 1861.[17]

The Bluchers also lived here long ago. I remember the colored woman, Phyllis, toting Miss Julia Blucher. Büsse[18] was an old German who lived on part of the Blucher place; he was a gunsmith. He had a lovely garden, with seedlings and plants of all kinds. My mother's calves would stray over near Büsse's place and when I would go after them I would look through the gate at the beautiful flowers. Mother taught me that it was all right to look at other people's flowers through the fence, but I must never reach my hand through to pick one. There were no roses in this garden; at that time there was only one rose bush in Corpus Christi and it was called the Rose of Castillo; it was pale pink and very fragrant. It grew on a great big bush in the yard of a Mexican woman, named Trinidad, living where Perkins' store is now.[19] Later Dr. Kearney bought some rose bushes and planted them around the customs house office on Chaparral Street.

The Lovenskiolds sent to Havana for roses for their garden, where they had many beautiful flowers. Col. Charles Lovenskiold

---

[15] Somers was Henry Kinney's nephew.

[16] Joseph Warren Kinney was Henry Kinney's brother. He was killed when his gun accidentally discharged, but Anna Moore could hardly have known him, since this happened in 1851, five years before she was born.

[17] Most accounts agree that Kinney was shot to death in Matamoros at the home of his ex-lover on March 3, 1862

[18] Frederick Büsse.

[19] The department store was at 701 Leopard at the Carancahua intersection.

paid Pat Dooley $300 a year, plus board and lodging, to take care of his garden. This was about 1867.

Col. Lovenskiold and William Gregory had under charter a boat, the *South American*, with Jim Nagle, Mrs. Gaffney's brother, as purser, and on one trip they brought a group of Irish servant girls here from New York. The Lovenskiolds took one (Charlotte), the Moores took one (Bridget), and the Headens took two. Pat Dooley married Charlotte.

The Woessners were also among the families living here in early days. William Woessner, a blacksmith, had four sons. One son, John, was a leading merchant and banker of Corpus Christi (Plate 12), and was the father of John, Walter, Anna, Ella, Blanche and Hattie. Another son, Martin, was a clerk in John's store, as well as in other stores, but did own a store of his own; he was sickly and died young. Another son, Charles Henry, married a young woman from Victoria or Goliad and had three daughters; his second wife was Miss Mollie Pettigrew. A fourth son, Willie, married a Miss Wilmot.

Old Dr. Eli Merriman, a prominent physician and ranchman, was a Congregationalist, although many thought he was an Episcopalian. His wife was a Miss Fusselman. They had a ranch near Banquete. One of the slaves there was Cynthy, a good friend of Mama's from the time she was about 18 years old. It was the custom in those days, when there were many slaves in a household, to divide the sewing according to what each woman could do best. Cynthy, who was a fine seamstress, made the shirt bosoms, stitching the shirt fronts, collars and cuffs. Her husband was Tom Randall.

One of the best-known citizens of Corpus Christi in those days was Judge Dickie Power. He has sometimes been confused with William Power, who came here after the Civil War and lived at the foot of the bluff for a while. After his marriage to a girl named Ellen, William Power bought a place on the bluff, the lot where Glover Johns lives now (about 309 South Broadway).

Dr. Spohn, a leading physician, had his first hospital at the home of Mrs. Culpepper, daughter of the Rev. Horace Clark. The second hospital was in the Hassell house, which was some distance out but not as far out as the Alta Vista Hotel (Plate 16), which was built later. A nurse for Dr. Spohn, well-remembered by many, was a Mexican woman, Nieves Verein, known as Chala.

Many Jews came here in early days but few of them observed any religious practices of their race. Joseph and Alfred Moses were brothers who had ranching interests near San Diego. Joseph died in Monterrey, leaving two daughters, Zara and Belle (Isabel), whose education had not been completed. Their uncle Alfred thought they should be further educated, and as plenty of money was available, he brought them from Monterrey and arranged for them to live with Mr. and Mrs. Perry Doddridge. The girls became Presbyterians, as were the Doddridges; but Miss Belle, who became Mrs. Barnes, is now an Episcopalian.

Mr. and Mrs. Edward Ohler came here in Kinney's time. Mr. Ohler, a storekeeper, built two houses on Water Street, both near where the Nueces Hotel is now. One was right east of the Shaw Building (which was where the Jones Building is now), and the other one, a two-story combination home and store building, in the next block north (Plate 6). The Ohlers left here and went to Indianola, as people from other parts of Texas were doing, also because business was booming there; and in Corpus Christi it was dull, and people gave this town the go-by.

There were three Italian musicians here, who played together — Frank Pelligrino, harpist, Billy Falvella, violinist, and "Tony," flutist. They were brought to Corpus Christi from Cuero by Mr. Kerr, who had opened the St. James Hotel. They made wonderful music, without a doubt. People here loved music very much, and in order to encourage this trio to remain in Corpus, they would employ them as often as possible. They would play a tune or two for 25 cents. You could often hear them playing about town. Falvella held his violin with the strings away from the body, his left hand being at his shoulder near his neck and the body of the instrument being between his own body and the strings. It is said that the name "Falvella" was spelled "Falvelle" when the young musician came here. Another good violinist was Theodore Lawrence.

Mr. William Mann and family, who were among the prominent early settlers, in Corpus Christi, had a beautiful residence on the bluff, but their first home was near the bay, about where the railroad track now runs down Cooper's Alley. The Virginia House, so-called because Mr. Mann was from Virginia, was the name given to the Mann store building and its surrounding small houses. The Virginia House was red and was frequently called Mann's red house. It was quite an establishment, covering an entire city block. The big house faced the east, at the front of the block, while around the north, west and south sides of the square were smaller houses, or rooms, in which merchants might stay while in Corpus Christi, and in which their ox-cart drivers could find shelter, the better houses being assigned to the merchants and buyers, and the rougher rooms to the people of less importance. Some rooms were also used for storing merchandise by those who brought goods in or took goods away. The wagons would come in and drive directly into the square, where traders, drivers and merchandise could find accommodations.

The main house was three stories in height and was the biggest house in the town. The first two stories were of brick and adobe, and the third was frame. The first floor was used for merchandise; the family lived on the second floor; and the third was used as a Masonic Hall. At the front of the ground floor there was a very large door, so that cars of freight could be run right in there after being loaded from the ships. The wharf, known as Mann's wharf, ran directly out this door. It wasn't very wide. A track on this wharf extended into the building; and on this, small flatcars loaded with the freight were pushed by men. They were really too heavy to be moved by men; and so, later, the spaces between the ties on the wharf were filled with timber and mules were used to haul the cars. Even this, however, was awkward, as the wharf was narrow. When my mother arrived in Corpus Christi on Jan. 1, 1849, this wharf and track were already there, she remembered well, for she was so crippled from rheumatism that she couldn't walk, and was put from the boat on one of those flatcars and rolled in to the house.

After the war the Virginia House was kept as a hotel. Later, the halls were rented for the first colored public school, and the girls in the school had to sweep the stairs. One day when I was helping sweep, I accidentally knocked against the door of the Masonic Hall

70

and it flew open. The room was painted pale blue, with a blue ceiling, and there was painted a G-compass and square. I was scared nearly to death and went running down the stairs. I saw Col. Moore and told him about it, and he just laughed. The reason I was so afraid was because I had heard so many stories of what Masons would do if anyone told any of their secrets. Gen. Harney was an active Mason, but I liked him because he dressed so well.

The Virginia House was finally torn down and its former location is now approximately Guth Park.[20] During the Civil War, a great many families went to Beeville and Goliad, among them the Mann family. After the war the Manns went to Galveston to live.

The Mann wharf was not the first wharf built here. John Riggs' father[21] built the first, down there where the Elks' building is now. It was a brush wharf, being made of sticks and brush with sand and cement in between, but was not successful as it kept washing through. Ohler's wharf was here, I think, before Mann's, and the Sidbury wharf was built later where Mann had his. Central Wharf wasn't built until about the '70s. The warehouse at the foot of Central Wharf was bonded, and owned by a man named Willett. The Cahills had a hotel across the street from the warehouse, on the west side of Water Street (Plate 15).

On the bluff, away at the south end of town, was where Miss Eliza Wilson lived. She was a popular young lady and went to all of the dances and to all places of amusement that others went to, although she had been blind since she was 12 years old. Her mother was a sister of Major Carroll and had married a second time, her husband being a Mr. Stringer, who had one son. They owned all of that land where the Furmans live now. After Mr. Stringer died, Miss Eliza, her mother, and her stepbrother continued living there.

There was a one-gable house at the south end of town, which the Rabbs[22] bought in 1867. The reason I feel sure of the date is because that was the year of the yellow fever here. I remember that

---

[20] Meaning Guth Park downtown, not the later South Guth or West Guth Park. The downtown Guth Park was across the street just north of the U&I Restaurant. It was sold about 1940 and today is a parking lot.

[21] Hiram Riggs, who died in 1855.

[22] John and Martha Rabb.

Betty Rabb had run away and married Charlie Gravis, and that her parents wouldn't speak to her after that. She was at Gravis's when the yellow fever broke out, and Gravis made his wife take the baby and go back to her mother and father for safety; and a reconciliation was effected. It was to that one-gable house that she went. Two more gables have been added, and it has been remodeled a good deal since the Rabbs occupied it. It is located at 801 S. Broadway.[23]

Col. Lovenskiold and family lived close in town. His home on the bluff was just a half block from Broadway at the top of the ravine; it is now the corner of Blucher and North Carancahua. At the front of that block, facing Broadway, is where Kinney is said to have lived. In later years, this location was the home of Hamp Bee.

North of this was the Britton home and north of that, on the corner of Broadway and Lipan, when my mother came, was a frame house, in which Major Chapman lived, who was connected with the United States Army post here. After the Chapmans, the Cooks lived there.[24] Mrs. Cook died there, and soon after, Mr. Cook died, leaving two children, Cora and Jack; these two children were taken by Mr. and Mrs. Richard Power, who lived across the street, where the Cathedral is now, and who had no children of their own. As a young lady, Cora Cook taught school here just after the Civil War, for a short while. She married Capt. Bennett, of the Union Army. Her little boy was named Richard for Judge Power. The Cook property was bought by a man named Daniel Dowd, who sold it to Capt. Mifflin Kenedy.

Capt. Kenedy's big house was built some time in 1885. Mrs. Kenedy lived in it for only three weeks, as she died in March 1885. When the house was torn down not long ago, some people were puzzled by what looked like a tunnel running from the main house to a smaller building in the yard. There was nothing mysterious about it, as it merely led from the house to the room where the acetylene gas was made.

---

[23] The house survives in Heritage Park, known as the Merriman-Bobys House today.
[24] The W.W. Chapman house was moved to South Carancahua and later torn down to build the Agnes and Laredo traffic exchange.

Across the street Judge Dickie Power owned two cottages facing on Broadway, where the Cathedral is now; he lived in the corner cottage. Mrs. Bray and daughter, Miss Eliza, roomed at the Power home, where Miss Eliza taught school in one of the front rooms during the Civil War. In this room, also, Catholic services were held, as vandals had done a great deal of damage to the small concrete church building by carrying off materials and breaking up some of the concrete blocks. These services may not have been regular church services; possibly they were rosary. The mantel was used as an altar, having a crucifix in the center with a vase of flowers on each side. Judge Joseph FitzSimmons read the services in Latin, no priest being available at this time. Mrs. Forbes Britton played the melodeon.

The second cottage was occupied from time to time by various people, including the Wachens, Byingtons, and Dr. Gillett, a Yankee doctor whose daughter, Ada, married Edwin Chamberlain, a brother of Mrs. Henrietta M. King. The Buckleys were living there in 1874; and shortly after that Mrs. Rabb built a beautiful home on that property (Plate 11).[25]

A little further north on Broadway was the Mann home, approximately where Congressman Kleberg's home[26] is now. It was two stories and had a cellar. It was all frame, and plastered inside, while the Britton house was made of shell concrete. The Baskins lived with the Manns.

Immediately north of Mann's, and just south of where the first Presbyterian Church was built later, was the Redmond cottage, where John Redmond and his first wife, Louisa Baskin, lived. At the corner of Broadway and Leopard, where the Nixon building is now, was the Fitzgerald home. It was a beautiful, two-and-half story building of frame construction, with a brick-lined cellar and

---

[25] This was called the Magnolia Mansion. It was later bought by Mifflin Kenedy for his son John G. Kenedy. The house served as a temporary hospital following the 1919 hurricane.

[26] The Henrietta King mansion.

nice dormer windows. The interior was lathed and plastered. Later on, the property was owned by the Meulys.[27]

At the corner of Broadway and Antelope, where the new post office is now, the Headens lived, just south of the Hickey house; the Ohlers lived there earlier. About the middle of this same block on Broadway was the E. J. Davis home. Some have said that part of it had been moved in from the Britton ranch, but it was not; it was built of new lumber. Maybe the stables or barns were of the old lumber.

I said Mrs. Britton was living in the Redmond cottage in 1862, and the reason I remember the date so well is on account of the bombardment of Corpus Christi, which was in 1862, and which I remember as clearly as if it were yesterday. My mother was living in a little frame house north of the old Cahill building on Water Street. After the warning had been received that the town would be bombarded, Mrs. Britton came for us with an ambulance and took us out to Judge Cody's in the Motts — Nuecestown. From there we could hear the sound of the cannon just as well as if we had been in town.

Judge Cody was not prepared for the crowd of people that arrived from town just before dark; there were no candles. People slept wherever they could, out under the trees. A few had blankets which they spread on the ground. This event stands out in my memory as one of the most miserable experiences I ever went through. All next day we had only black coffee, buttermilk and cornbread to eat. It was the first time I had ever eaten cornbread made with buttermilk and soda, and the first time I had ever had coffee, as I had had only milk with hot water and sugar before that. The Codys were Irish and their brogue amused me, as I had never heard it before.

Next day, as there seemed to be no excitement in town, we came back, but went out to Judge Cody's again before night. It was

---

[27] Union occupation troops ripped out the house's window frames and doorways for firewood. Margaret Meuly later filed a claim with the government for damages.

reported that one man was killed, but I don't know anything about it.[28]

People in Corpus Christi suffered intensely during the Civil War, as food was very scarce. Persons of independent means, however, such as many of the ranchers, did not fare so badly. The Confederate commissary was established at Banquete, on account of the federals' activity at Corpus Christi, and this made it easier to obtain supplies out there. We were in Corpus Christi at the time of the bombardment, but soon after went to the George Evans ranch at Barranco Blanco, near Banquete, where we had everything we wanted and hardly knew there was a war.

After the war everybody had to take the ironclad oath in order to vote. I'm going to give the library this copy of the oath, that was signed by Thomas Fitzpatrick. (In library, Corpus Christi collection.) Thomas was an ex-slave. He and his sister Clara had belonged to Gen. Fitzpatrick, an Irishman who already had the title of "general" when he came to the United States. When the war came on, he wanted no part in it, so he went away, leaving Thomas with Judge Dickie Power and Clara with Mr. George Noessel, who had been a baron in Europe, and who was the father of Felix, Otto and Sophia Noessel. There was a brother of Thomas's who went off with Gen. Fitzpatrick. Thomas was called Tom Power here by everybody who knew him, because he belonged to Judge Power, but he never called himself that as he wanted to keep his old name of Fitzpatrick. After Thomas died, the man who looked after his papers gave my daughter, Adelaide, certain things that Thomas had wanted her to have.

One of the customs of the early days was for a family having large grounds at their home to have a burial plot in the yard, or to use the garden to bury the dead. Several members of the Mann, Baskin and Redmond families were buried at the rear of the Mann home. Joe Armstrong, too, was buried there. This would be where the Kleberg garage is now, on North Carancahua Street, but that street had not been open then. The body of Mr. Mann was buried a little to the north of the others, and it was removed in later years to

---

[28] One Confederate soldier, Pvt. Henry Moat, was killed.

lie beside that of his wife in old Bayview Cemetery, where their graves are marked by a double monument. Old Mr. Redmond, the doctor's father, was buried in the Mann private plot, too; I don't know whether his body and the bodies of the others buried there were ever removed.

Another large burial plot was that at the rear of the Doddridge home on South Bluff. A small daughter of Mr. and Mrs. Felix Blucher, Anne Elizabeth, was buried in their yard; the body was later removed to old Bayview Cemetery. This child, I think, was named for Mrs. Britton's daughter, Anne Elizabeth, as the Bluchers and Brittons were close friends. A little Cahill child named Ellen was buried where the new Catholic Cathedral is now. There was a Merriman[29] family who lost all of their children with yellow fever, I think it was. He was a lawyer and his wife was related to Col. Henry Kinney. The children were buried in the yard of their home, located somewhere between South Carancahua and South Tancahua, north of Kinney Avenue.

In the yellow fever epidemic of 1867, many lives were lost, and Corpus Christi would have been swept as clean as a pin if it hadn't been for E. J. Davis's bringing Dr. Kearney[30] here from Havana at his own expense after the three doctors — Dr. Merriman, Dr. Robertson and Dr. Johnson — had all died of the fever. Many mean things have been said about Mr. Davis, but he certainly deserves credit for what he did for Corpus Christi at that time.

Dr. Kearney, a celebrated physician, had his hands full looking after the sick. His treatment consisted of having the patient put his feet into a mustard bath up to the knees, and then go to bed, where he was given warm teas of any kind. For nourishment he was given clabber, or the whey from boiled buttermilk. Dr. Kearney didn't use as much whisky in treating yellow fever as the other doctors did.

So many people died that the lumber that was on hand to build the Presbyterian Church had to be used for coffins. The bodies of the dead were hauled to the cemetery in drays; and as there wasn't

---

[29] Walter Merriman.

[30] Dr. Thomas Kearney, who later served as quarantine officer.

time to dig deep graves they were buried very shallow, only about four feet deep.

I remember the death of Dr. Johnson's[31] baby, only eight months old. One day when I took the baby's clothes to Mrs. Johnson the baby was sick with the fever. Mrs. Johnson put it in my arms, and it died while I held it. She took it from me and laid it on the bed. But I didn't take the fever. Mrs. Johnson also escaped.

Dr. Robertson[32] had a drug store in Corpus Christi. He was the father of Mrs. Jessie Clark and Mrs. Eli Merriman, and lived at the corner of Chaparral and Schatzell streets, where Lichtenstein's store is.[33] Dr. Kearney stayed in Corpus Christi until Dr. Spohn came in the early 1870s. Dr. Spohn, an army doctor, and Dr. Kearney became great friends, and even after Dr. Kearney left here to live on his sheep ranch near Laredo he would visit Dr. Spohn every time he came back to Corpus. I never heard of any relatives. I think he was a Republican.

Dr. Kearney lived on Chaparral Street, about three houses south of where Penney's is now (corner of Chaparral and Starr), in a little cottage that the DeRyees owned later. He was connected with the customs office here. He sent to Havana and got four rose bushes that he planted in his front yard, two on each side. They were so sweet you could smell their fragrance when you reached that street. The plants were so vigorous and hardy that even the coldest weather didn't kill them. These famous Kearney roses were cabbage roses, very large, and were much in demand by the young men of the town, who wanted them to take to their sweethearts.

It was a number of years before we had another yellow fever scare, and it was only a scare; that was in 1873. Very much later, in 1897, there was another scare here. Two cases were reported in San Antonio and one here; but the case in Corpus Christi couldn't be found. Many people left, going to different places. Saltillo, especially, was popular to go to, and a number of families,

---

[31] Dr. G. F. Johnston.

[32] Dr. George Robertson.

[33] This was the third Lichtenstein location; the final location was one block down and across the street, at the corner of Chaparral and Lawrence.

including the Weils, went there. But the scare passed over very soon.

I often think about the schools in those early days. I attended the convent first. I went also to Mr. Rowe, the Congregational minister,[34] and to Mrs. Bray, Mrs. Peterson's mother. After the Civil War I was in Mrs. John Dix's[35] school a while. And then I went for three weeks to the public school; this was the colored school held in the halls of the Virginia House in 1873. Mr. Lacy, a white man, was the first principal. Later on, when there were about 40 pupils in this school, a lady assistant, Mrs. Barnes, helped. She was the mother of Ben Barnes and had come here with her mother from Rockport. Mr. Lacy received some school lots in part payment for his services, as there wasn't any money. Another teacher who received land was Mrs. Conklin. As Capt. King had given the land for school purposes, with the provision that it was to revert to him if not so used, it was thought all right to use it for paying the teachers.

The first building put up for a public school was built on the hill on some property given by Capt. King. It was the same location used now for a school, between Carancahua and Tancahua streets. A two-story building, with four rooms on each floor, was built for white children, and a two-room building south of this for the colored pupils. In this small building several classes were held in the large room. Mr. Lacy continued as principal, and Mrs. Barnes as assistant, although after about two sessions Mrs. Barnes was persuaded to give up her public school work in order to teach music. Later, a third room was added to the little school house. After the new school was built for colored pupils, this one-story building was used as the high school for white pupils. The second colored school principal was Solomon M. Coles.

---

[34] The white chaplain of the 122nd U.S. Infantry, Rev. Aaron Rowe, established the Freedom Congregational Church, the first church for African-Americans in Corpus Christi.

[35] A school for girls was operated in the Dix home on Water Street by Mary Eliza Hayes Dix. She taught black girls sewing in the morning and white girls standard academic subjects in the afternoon. His daughter kept school for the children of former slaves.

I remember that Mrs. Conklin had a private school before she was married. She was then Miss Hannah Moore. At her home, Mrs. Conklin was fond of entertaining, and she was hostess at times to different noted women, one of whom was a famous singer named Bell.

Thinking of all these days gone by, recalls to my mind the story of something that happened in the old Fitzgerald home at Broadway and Leopard. During the Civil War this house was abandoned. Vandals had entered and damaged it badly, as it continued unoccupied. One time, probably in the early 1870s, an old man from Mexico came along and established himself in the second story of that house, cooking in the basement. He seemed to be of Spanish descent and had a good education, but was in abject poverty. People thought he was a political exile.

An ex-United States soldier from some place along the border came to Corpus Christi and picked up a living working for people in the yards. The pay at that time was $1 a day — anybody was glad to get that much, and a person had no trouble getting help at that price. This man, old Charlie, also went to the old Fitzgerald house to stay. He struck up a sort of bargain with the old Mexican, who was named Flores, according to which the Mexican would cook for him, and for this work he would receive his board, and 50 cents a week for cigarettes, etc. This kept up for quite a while.

One Saturday night when Charlie came home with his six dollars — the week's wages — old Flores asked him for one dollar. Charlie said, "I have made a bargain with you, and you were to get only 50 cents a week; that's all I'm going to give you." And he wouldn't give Flores any more.

Next morning a group of small boys, on their way to the Presbyterian Sunday School nearby, stopped at the old house, as was their custom, and whistled, called, and chirped as usual just to plague the old Mexican man and hear him swear violently in a number of languages. But all was silent that morning. Several of the boys ran up to the second floor ahead of the others; still all was quiet. The others gathered then, and they began to look around for the man. One of the boys, maybe Willie Woessner, for he was usually a ringleader in the boys' mischief, opened a closet door, and out fell a dead man, with a deep gash in his stomach. Some of the boys leaped out the windows in their fright; and the others rushed down the stairs and called people to come and see. Old Charlie had been murdered.

A great hunt was made for the missing Mexican man. After some days he was found nearly starved, hiding out at Avery Point. As the men approached him, he said, "I know what you want me for, for killing Charlie. Well, I'll go with you, but I'll never hang for it. If it were known what all I've done, there isn't a limb of a tree that would refuse to take my neck. But I'm not going to hang."

Flores was put in a cell, like a cage, in the jail, in the old courthouse. He spent his time writing poetry in Spanish, which he would hand out to different persons here and there, and in making beautiful designs for embroidering, and was very well liked. He wasn't kept in the cage in the daytime, but at night he would be locked in. One night the weather became very cold and there was a severe freeze. Next morning the old man was found dead in his cell. He was right. He didn't hang.

I have heard many stories of the early days in Corpus Christi, for mother and her friends used to enjoy telling about them. Two of her especial friends were Aunt Anne and Uncle Dempsey. Aunt Anne was French, and very fine-looking. Uncle Dempsey had bought two lots on Tancahua Street and when the Jones claim was active, he was told he would have to pay $20 for the corner lot and $15 for the other one. His friends counseled him not to pay, as he had already bought the lots once. But he said that the Jones claim went way back, and he thought he had better pay. He did; and later events showed his wisdom, as many other people had to pay many times what he did to secure the title to their property.[36]

I always listened with great interest to the tales of the old folks, as they related the incidents that occurred in the families whom they had served. Mother was especially fond of speaking about the days

---

[36] Land purchased by Henry L. Kinney from Enrique Villarreal in 1842 was later claimed by Galveston land speculator Dr. Levi Jones. After decades of litigation, the case was decided in favor of the Jones' claimants and landowners in Corpus Christi had to repurchase their property to obtain clear title to their holdings.

she spent at the Britton Ranch at the Oso. Mr. Britton would serve sherry when company would come, and mother was always pleased to put on a fresh apron and carry in the tray with the wine.

Among the friends who came to the ranch frequently was Mr. Jesse P. Perham. He was a Methodist minister, and I have been told he had a sheep ranch at Banquete. One day Mr. Perham said to Mr. Britton, "Why don't you enjoy life out here? If I had all this I surely would enjoy myself."

"Why," said Mr. Britton, "I do enjoy life very much. I enjoy life immensely."

"Well," said Mr. Perham, "do you want to know what I would do if I lived here?" And he looked at the big windmill with its lazily moving wings. "I would have a rocking chair set up there underneath those wings and I would whistle Yankee Doodle as the cattle came to water."

I remember hearing about the Methodists raising money for a church, too. The Rev. Lafferty was their preacher, and the congregation asked him to help them build a church. Mr. Lafferty went to "old man Peter Dunn"[37] (the Dunns were Catholics) and said to him, "Mr. Dunn, I want your help. These people want me to build them a church, and I'm not well-enough acquainted with everybody here to do this. Mr. Dunn, we're of the same race, though not of the same religion, but we're all going to the same heaven. Will you help me?"

Mr. Dunn said, "Wait until I finish beating this horseshoe and I'll see what I can do." And he finished beating the horseshoe and tossed it into a bucket of cold water, took his coat off a nail and put it on and said, "Come along."

They went to the door of the Favorite Saloon,[38] which was later George Roberts' saloon, and Mr. Dunn said to the men inside, "Now, men, this man is trying to build a church for the people here, and he needs some help to get this thing started. I want each of you to put the price of your next drink in this hat for the church." The

---

[37] This was Peter Dunne, who had a blacksmith shop on Water Street, called "Uncle Peter."

[38] On Chaparral Street, next door to the Crescent Hotel.

men stepped up and each contributed something. That was how the Methodist Church building got started; that was before the Civil War. This first building was a small adobe one-story building facing south on Mann Street, about the middle of the block.

There were so many good people in those days. It makes me sad when I see people hating each other as some do, even members of the same family harboring bitterness in their hearts against each other. The parable of the Good Samaritan is a good example to follow. I say — "Be a Good Samaritan." You can't go to heaven with hatred in your heart.

Anna Moore Schwien (1856-1946). Her mother Malvina was one of the first slaves in Corpus Christi. She arrived in 1849 with the Baskin family from Mississippi. When the business partnership of Baskin, Mann and Britton was dissolved and the property divided, Malvina was left to Capt. Britton, whom she served as a house servant. Britton went into a sheep-raising venture with George Wilkins Kendall near New Braunfels, where Malvina was sent at the time of Anna's birth in 1856. (The unusual circumstances of Anna's birth on a remote sheep ranch suggest the possibility she was the daughter of slave Malvina and her master Forbes Britton, as suggested in a column by Murphy Givens on April 10, 2013.) Anna and her mother returned to Corpus Christi when she was four years old. Her mother married Sam Moore, a slave of Col. John M. Moore. After the Civil War, Anna was educated in a school conducted by Mrs. John Dix (in the house later converted into the Seaside Hotel) and by Rev. Aaron Rowe, a Congregation minister who ran a school for the children of former slaves. Anna became a teacher in Negro schools. In 1881, when she was 26, she married a German immigrant named C. W. Schweine, who was driven out of town because he married a black woman. She never remarried and kept her husband's name for the rest of her life. Dates of interview by Marie Blucher from Nov. 8, 1938 to May 15, 1941. Anna Moore Schwien died on the eve of her 90th birthday, on April 19, 1946.

CHAPTER 5

ELI T. MERRIMAN
REMINISCENCES

My father was a doctor and ranchman. He practiced medicine in the Rio Grande Valley in the 1840s and 1850s, and it was there I was born in 1852. He moved to Banquete in 1857 because it was a great horse-trading center and more convenient to the trade. My mother's name was Elizabeth Fusselman.

In 1864 I was sent to Corpus Christi to go to school. I boarded at John Riggs' home on Chaparral Street, and the next year the family moved to Corpus. Father didn't give up his practice in Banquete but maintained an office and hospital there.

Father bought some property on Chaparral Street, near where Kress's store is now.[1] Here we lived for many years in a small cottage. There was a big cannonball in the yard from the time the federals bombarded the town; but we had heard so many stories about these balls being unexploded, and especially a tale about one of them exploding in Galveston, that mother paid someone to take ours and drop it in the bay. Much later, I paid Ed Crockett one dollar to recover the cannonball from the water, and for many years after this it lay in the yard of my home on Water Street. During the hurricane of 1919 it became buried in the sand, but I dug it out and took it out to my daughter's house in Nueces Bay Heights, where I

---

[1] The Kress store was at 619 North Chaparral.

was living for a while, and had it out in the front yard. One morning I noticed it was missing, and have never seen it since. Someone must have taken it.

In the early days there were two drug stores here, Dr. Robertson's[2] and Dr. DeRyee's. The former was patronized by one of the physicians — Dr. Merriman, my father — while DeRyee's drug store was patronized by the other physician, Dr. Johnson.[3]

I think Dr. William DeRyee came from Alsace-Lorraine. He was a chemist, although he had a great interest in mining, with many ideas on the subject, and I believe he owned shares in some mines out West. His real hobby was collecting rocks and minerals, many of which he gathered near Sharpsburg in San Patricio County. On one of his trips, there was a sudden freshet that unexpectedly formed a body of water about two miles wide across the flats, and caught Dr. DeRyee on the other side. But this didn't dismay him. He got two barrels, fastened them together, and sat between the barrels with a pair of oars; and in this way paddled himself across the shallow water until he arrived at the Motts (Nuecestown) on this side of the bay.

Dr. DeRyee had the idea that there was something valuable under the ground over there. And he was right, because now it is a big oil and gas field. He was also fond of all forms of wildlife. He had quite a collection of mounted specimens in his drugstore window,[4] among them an alligator, an eel, leeches, and a duck with its bill clamped in an oyster shell.

Among the old buildings here that have been torn down was Belden and Gilpin's old concrete warehouse at the corner of Laguna and Chaparral streets, built in 1849. The Ranahan house (later called the FitzSimmons house) that stood on Chaparral Street, north of the Ritz Theater was another one, built very early, probably about 1848. A hole was torn in this house during the bombardment of Corpus Christi in 1862.

---

[2] Dr. George Robertson.

[3] Other sources spell it as Dr. G. F. Johnston.

[4] The DeRyee drugstore was at the corner of Chaparral and Peoples; the City National Bank was later built on that site.

Still standing is a house at the corner of Taylor and Chaparral streets which was built before either of the other two. According to John J. Dix — and he ought to know — it was used as a commissary for Zachary Taylor's army. And after the Civil War it was there that the ironclad oath of allegiance was signed.[5]

The Meuly house on Chaparral Street, built about 1852 or 1853, and the Wrather house on the same street, built after I came to Corpus Christi, are still standing.[6] A man named Dwyer built the first house on the bluff; I don't recall his first name, but his father[7] had a horse ranch in San Patricio County.

There were several pairs of houses that were so near each other and looked so much alike that it was striking. On Water Street, facing east at the opposite corners of Water and Peoples, were the two-story Hunsaker and Ohler buildings (Plate 6). On Broadway, the Pettigrew house at the corner of Leopard Street and the Holbein house at the corner of Antelope, were very much alike. On Tancahua was the Parker house and beside it the Hidalgo Seminary, both two-story concrete buildings.

The Bidwell hotel was built by M. Blumenthal, though it was not known as the Bidwell when built.[8] Another landmark of the town now gone was the Market Hall (Plate 25) that stood until it was torn down to make way for a new City Hall under the administration of Mayor Clark Pease, a very progressive leader. The bell in old Market Hall was depended on by the people to set their clocks, to go to work and school by, and for fire and all other alarms. On New Year's eve of 1938-1839, Tom Cahill and I went and rang this same old bell. It is mounted on a cement base right back of the City Hall, where the fire boys sit under the grapevine. I tell you, someone ought to write up about that vine; it is wonderful,

---

[5] This was known as the Russell place, then the Ironclad Oath house, then it became the Royal Givens home. It was located at 802 Chaparral.

[6] The Meuly house on Chaparral was torn down to make way for a Fedway store; on that site today is the Education Service Center. The Wrather house was at 912 Chaparral. The family lived upstairs over a store on the first floor.

[7] Thomas Dwyer, a barrister in England, moved to the Corpus Christi area in 1848 and started a horse and mule ranch.

[8] First named the Constantine Hotel.

so big, spreading over that huge trellis. The bell, of course, can't be pulled back and forth as it used to be rung, but you can move the clapper and make it sound.

There were three main streets in Corpus when I was a boy, running north and south below the bluff; they were Chaparral, Mesquite and Water streets. But no one used the names of Chaparral and Mesquite; they were called Front and Back streets. Even Back street wasn't mentioned much. It was mainly Front Street and Water Street that we spoke of.

The cross streets were named after leading citizens, such as Lawrence, Belden, Peoples, Mann, Aubrey, William, Doddridge; later Blucher and Kinney were added, the former for Major Blucher, officer in the Confederate Army, and the latter for Colonel Kinney, founder of Kinney's Trading Post. On the hill, many of the streets running north and south were named for tribes of Indians, while several of those running east and west were given the names of animals.

Speaking of names, it was a strange thing that there was nobody here named Smith or Jones or Brown, in those days; but there were plenty of other names duplicated, so that to distinguish one from another we spoke of "Baker" Allen and "Shoemaker" Allen, "Tinner" Hall and "Butcher" Hall. The first Smith to live in Corpus Christi was John Smith, the carpenter.

The first school I attended was the Hidalgo Seminary, one of the biggest schools in this part of the state. It was for boys only and pupils came from Laredo, Victoria, Goliad, and many other towns of South Texas. It was managed by the Catholic church, with Father Gonnard at the head, and was located in a concrete building on the edge of an arroyo long since filled up, where North Tancahua and Lipan streets now meet. Father Gonnard didn't teach me himself, but he would come to the schoolroom and give talks to the pupils.

One of the teachers under Father Gonnard was a man called "Little" Carroll,[9] brother of Charles Carroll of the firm of Carroll &

---

[9] William Carroll, whose niece, Mary Carroll, would later become superintendent of schools and a high school was named for her. William's brother and Mary Carroll's father was Charles Carroll, architect.

Iler, builders. Father Gonnard died in the yellow fever epidemic in 1867. Robert Dougherty next headed the school, and later Mr. Campion was in charge. The school closed when the Legislature established public schools, about 1870.

Twelve or 15 years ago, John Gallagher and I made up a list of men who had attended Hidalgo Seminary, who were still living; there were 108. Now I know of only eight, and three of them are Merrimans: my brother John C., of Laredo, and my brother George, of Muskogee, and myself; Willie Rankin; Ambrose Priour; Clark Denton; Andy Anderson; and John Dunn.

For a while I went to Allen's school, in the downstairs part of the Conrad Meuly building on Chaparral. Another school I went to was Professor McOmber's, up there in the old Methodist Church building. One day at recess I went down to Judge Neal's publishing office to see if I could get a job, and I did. I quit school and began working there next morning. This was in 1870 and was the beginning of my newspaper career. Judge Neal at this time was publishing the *Nueces Valley*.

E. J. Davis, when governor of Texas, bought the *Nueces Valley* and made it one of the official organs of the state, which of course meant it was Republican. Bill Maltby was then publishing the *Advertiser*, and as Gov. Davis's paper had to be used for all official notices, Maltby lost a great deal of the advertising he had been carrying. This situation angered not only the publisher but many of the advertisers as well. Finally, after Davis lost out, the merchants got together and bought the *Nueces Valley*. This paper in 1872 had a Washington hand press and a little Liberty job press, which Maltby bought in New York, and its office was up over Atwood's tin shop.

The merchants who bought the *Nueces Valley* were referred to as the "anti-monopoly" group, as opposed to the "wharf monopoly" group, which comprised those persons supporting the Central Wharf & Warehouse Company's activities. A leader of the anti-monopoly group was Norwick Gussett; another was Charles Beaman, who published the paper for a while. Mr. Gussett built his own wharf outside the city limits[10] because he was angry at not being taken into the Central Wharf & Warehouse Company (Plate 15). His campaign, which was supported by all the Jews as well as many others, was very successful; he did a big business, and had his own fleet of boats. The usual dray charge was 25 cents a trip, but Gussett's charge was 37 and one-half cents, because he was out of the city limits.[11] Gussett's opposition caused the Central Wharf & Warehouse Company, which had been paying the city $1,000 a month from their wharfage and other income, to quit making these payments which had guaranteed their monopoly. Then anybody who wanted to build a wharf could do so.

To go back to E. J. Davis — he had law offices in the old Hunsaker building in the 1860s, being associated with J. B. Murphy. Davis was a tall, red-whiskered man. He married the daughter of Forbes Britton and they lived on Broadway near where the post office is now; but after Davis's term as governor, they sold their home and never came back to live in Corpus Christi.

Davis wasn't popular here because of his political activities. He was elected governor because the Republicans threw out a good many counties in the counting of votes. Many Democrats couldn't even sign the oath of allegiance, required for voting, and by throwing out some of the counties sufficient votes were obtained to elect Davis.

During the Civil War, when Davis nearly lost his life in Brownsville, it was the Masons who saved him, they say. When I was in Galveston in 1874 I saw a locomotive with the name of E. J. Davis on it.

I was asked once if I remembered Ira H. Evans. Yes, I remember him well. It must have been about 1872 when he boarded at mother's.[12] He was a Republican, a jolly, middle-aged man; and I can even now see him nearly double up laughing at Jim Luby's famous stories, which I, as a boy, enjoyed listening to. I believe Mr.

---

[10] Off North Beach.

[11] E. H. Caldwell said Gussett's wharf and warehouse were located where the Breakers Hotel was built.

[12] Merriman's widowed mother operated a popular boarding house on Mesquite Street.

88

Evans was unmarried, and he seemed to be connected with the customs office here.

On Christmas nights a bunch of us used to shoot fireworks out west of the place. There were Charlie DeRyee, Andy Anderson, Charlie, George and Dick Blucher, and many others. Charlie Gravis played the melodeon behind the door in the Methodist Church, the church that faced west. The minister was Mr. Cox;[13] you sure could *hear* him preach. At that time the men were seated on one side of the church and the women on the other.

In 1867 there was an epidemic of yellow fever here; it was a terrible thing, with so many dying each day. My father, who was one of the few doctors here, died of the fever. I didn't take it, and I guess the reason was that I had been well-dosed by my father for a slight illness not long before the epidemic began.

It was along about the 1870s, I think, that the Pioneer Fire Company was organized. This was followed by the Hook and Ladder Company. Then these two groups joined and became the Corpus Christi Fire Department. Later there were also three or four hose companies.[14]

Another company organized in the 1870s was the Star Rifles, but it was not formed until after the Mexican raid in March 1875, for it was this raid that led to its organization. The captain was S. T. Foster and E. P. Hill was lieutenant; another officer was a man named Heldenfels. I was a charter member. We had bright new uniforms and used to drill up at Artesian Park. This was the first company of Star Rifles ever to exist here, and it was not possible that the Star Rifles ran out on the wharf at the time of the Mexican raid, as had been alleged. This company was later disbanded and shortly afterwards, I think, another company of Star Rifles, composed of different men, was organized.

Another thing I remember as happening in the 1870s was the building of the Tex-Mex railroad. It was started as the Corpus

---

[13] Rev. A.F. Cox.

[14] Joining the Pioneer Fire Company No. 1 and Lone Star Hook & Ladder Company were the Protection Hose Company No. 2, Security Hose Company No. 3, and Shamrock Hose Company No. 4.

Christi, San Diego and Rio Grande Narrow Gauge Railway. The first spike for the first railroad in South Texas was driven over there about where the Corpus Christi Hardware Company is now,[15] where the end of the track used to be for many years. At the ceremony, held on Thanksgiving Day of 1876, Mr. Rogers, the Methodist preacher, delivered the prayer, and William Headen, mayor, gave the address. The spike, which had been gilded by James McKenzie, was driven by Uriah Lott, ties and rails having been already laid in place. During the following night the spike disappeared.

Grading was started west of the Blucher residence. I made this statement a long time ago, and about 10 years ago J. P. Nelson verified what I had said. Nelson had wanted the contract for grading, but Lott told him they already had a man grading out west of Blucher's place. Nelson investigated and found only one man with a pick and shovel and wheelbarrow. A contract was then worked out for Nelson to take over the work, and he graded the road all the way to Laredo. He married Amanda Myers and they lived in San Antonio.

When the first trains began running they got their water from a well in the arroyo, using a bucket to fill the water tank. This had to last until they reached Oso Creek, where a big dam across the stream provided plenty of water. The next point where they could get water was at Agua Dulce Creek at Banquete.

There was a little town known as Collins about four or five miles east of the present city of Alice, but as the new railroad didn't pass through Collins the town dwindled away until there is hardly anything there now. The building of the railroad didn't displace the older forms of transportation all at once. I remember riding on King and Kenedy's stage line to Brownsville in 1882 and seeing many teams coming along the road. It was many years before a railroad connected Brownsville and Corpus.

Someone asked me about the Myrtle Club. Well, although I wasn't a member, I recall that this club used the south part of the upstairs floor of the Doddridge Building (Plate 19) for their clubroom. I think that was probably in the early 1880s. The club

---

[15] At 99 South Broadway.

was composed of society people, men only I think. I remember that the Myrtle Club room was used for a big gathering of businessmen held to meet John Garner just after he was elected to Congress. Garner wanted to show his gratitude for his election, and to find out what this part of his constituency wished him to do for them in Congress. Hugh Sutherland's father got up and voiced the sentiments of the entire group when he said they wanted a straight channel dredged right through Turtle Cove. Garner went on to Congress. He introduced a channel bill. He wired the news that the channel would be dug. Later, Garner got President Taft to come to Corpus Christi through the new 13-foot channel.

In 1874, when I came back from Galveston, I was with Frank Barnard in publishing the *Advertiser.* Beaman was running the *Nueces Valley.* Frank Barnard told me one time he couldn't pay me $12 a week any longer and so I was without a job. Bill Maltby and I established the *Free Press* in 1877. Maltby stayed in the office and I was the outside man. After his death I bought his widow's share for $1,500.

In 1882, I went to California on a visit, leaving Jim Holterhaus and Doc Berry in charge, with J. P. Caruthers (brother-in-law of James Fulton, brother of George Fulton) as editor. When I returned I found that Caruthers and Ed Williams, another newspaper man, had been talking to Capt. King and Capt. Kenedy about starting a new paper to be known as the *Caller*, which King and Kenedy were going to back. They wanted to know if I would join in with them; that is, sell them my paper. I didn't want to, but was advised to do so because of the fact that if King and Kenedy were to back the new paper I wouldn't have a chance with the *Free Press* any longer. So I sold them the *Free Press* for $2,500 and went in with them in publishing the *Caller*. This name was selected after Mr. Caruthers mentioned a paper in California called the *San Francisco Call*. We liked the name *Call*, but didn't want to use exactly the same form as the San Francisco paper, and so we named our paper the *Caller*. The significance we attached to this name was that as newsboys called out the paper for sale, the hearer would get the conception of the paper being a caller of news, just as in earlier times a town crier would cry out the news.

There was another paper here at that time, a semi-weekly published by the Barnards, called the *Ledger*, which although smaller had better presses than the *Free Press*. King and Kenedy bought the *Ledger*, too, and moved everything to the Noessel building at the corner of Chaparral and William streets. The first issue of the *Caller* came out in January 1883.

Each year at New Year's we always published a Carrier's Address, which was a full-page poem printed on separate sheets of paper and given by the *Caller* carriers to their patrons, who would usually give the boy a dime. Old Dickie Power was author of most of our carrier's addresses. He would spend two or three weeks writing up one of these poems. Thoughts came to him by inspiration and he would leave whatever he was doing to jot them down; he would even rush in from the woodpile, where he was chopping wood, to put down some idea that had just come to him for his poem. His last address was incomplete when he died, and so I used parts of an older one he had written to finish it out.

Dickie Power wrote lots of poetry and his poems were just splendid. There was another poet here, a man named Carroll. He and Mr. Power were both Irish and were jealous of each other. Carroll always wrote about poor old Ireland. Dickie Power's home on the bluff had little windows on account of the Indians. He had an adopted boy who played the violin.

Ed Williams ran for mayor in 1882 against the advice of friends, who told him he wouldn't be elected. When Capt. Kenedy, whose office was right across the street from the *Free Press*, heard of it he was very angry. He didn't think Williams should go into politics when he was connected with the paper and he determined to see that Williams wasn't elected. He spent lots of money on the hill, and Williams was defeated by his opponent, J. B. Murphy. Williams then went to Mexico and engaged in mining and later moved to the City of Mexico, where he was killed in a streetcar accident.

Judge B. F. Neal, our first mayor, was in the newspaper business here in 1870. Henry Maltby published the *Ranchero* in 1859; later he went to Brownsville where he continued the same paper for a number of years. His wife was a Miss Franks. Their son,

David, lives in Brownsville now. Bill Maltby, brother of Henry, was another Corpus Christi pioneer; he published the *Advertiser* after the war. He married Mrs. Swift's daughter, Grace. Jasper Maltby was a son of Bill.

Altogether there have been about 25 newspapers published in Corpus Christi. There were the *Star*, the *Critic*, the *Gazette*, the *Advertiser,* the *Ranchero*, the *Times*, the *Nueces Valley* (this was published before the war, and then after the war it resumed publication), and many others. One of the early publishers was a man named Bryant; when I was a boy I knew his two sons and their sister, who lived in the St. James Hotel. The three children all wrote poetry, and the girl had several books of her poems published.

About 1889 or 1890 Col. E. H. Ropes came to Corpus and started a big real estate boom. He built the beautiful Alta Vista Hotel (Plate 16), which burned a good many years ago. Unfortunately a money panic came along in the early 1890s and the boom collapsed.

I knew a lawyer named Miller, active here at the time of the Ropes boom, who told me this story of Gen. Zachary Taylor. Mr. Miller roomed at the Belden house, corner of Laguna and Mesquite streets, and Mrs. Belden told him many stories of the days when Gen. Taylor was encamped here with the army.

At that time there was only a little long frame building at the Belden corner. Belden and Gilpin's concrete warehouse stood away back from the street. Mr. Belden, whose sister married J. B. Mitchell, was among the leading citizens here and frequently entertained notables at his home. On one occasion Gen. Taylor was his guest. He told of his plans to go to Mexico City, and promised to bring Mrs. Belden a silk dress from the city. Mrs. Belden said to him, "You'll never get there."

"Yes, I will," the general replied. "Remember the Alamo." Gen. Taylor never returned to Corpus Christi, but he sent the promised silk dress to Mrs. Belden from Mexico by someone else. Mr. Miller told me he saw the dress. Mrs. Belden was a Mexican woman,[16] but

---

[16] Her maiden name was Mauricia Arocha. She lived in Matamoros when she met and married Frederick Belden in 1831.

at that time it was not as unusual as it is now, for a prominent man to have a Mexican wife, as many of the early settlers had married Mexican or Spanish women. Mrs. Belden was a very dark-skinned woman; she was unusually smart and was quite well-known because of her husband's wealth and importance to the town.

Some of Zachary Taylor's soldiers are buried in old Bayview Cemetery. This is the oldest cemetery in this part of the state of Texas, except, perhaps, the one at Banquete. Many of the victims of the yellow fever epidemic of 1867 are buried there, too. My family are buried there and that's where I shall lie when I have joined them beyond the river. You know, that's one of my favorite hymns. At night, if I can't go to sleep, I just sing that old song, "Shall we gather at the river?" and I soon drop off to sleep.

CIVIL WAR REMINISCENCES

The federals, or Yankees, as the Confederates called them in those days (the federals calling the Confederates rebels), made frequent visits to Corpus Christi or to the waters of the bay in their scouting trips about Aransas Pass as well as Corpus Christi Pass during the early 1860s.

They came to Corpus Christi once too often in 1862 when Captain Kittredge said he came to bombard the town and capture the place, but instead of capturing it, got captured himself. Major Felix Blucher, father of Charles and George Blucher, fired the first cannon, Herman Meuly says, from the Confederate battery on North Beach, taking the federals by surprise by sending a ball right through one of their ships.

Among the Confederates in the trenches on the waterfront east of the Giles Hotel[17] was Lt. John S. Brown, father of W. B. Brown, of this city. Kittredge, who was captured down at Flour Bluff after the battle, visited the home of Col. Charles Lovenskiold on the bluff during one of his trips, sticking his bayonet through the

---

[17] 1107 North Chaparral.

clothing in the wardrobe, thinking possibly the colonel might be hiding there, says his daughter, Mrs. Alice Rankin, who was present, and who heard her mother tell Capt. Kittredge that he had better look in the cistern, which remark made him angry and he left the premises.

At another time it is said Mrs. Lovenskiold entertained some of the Yankee soldiers, giving them cake and wine to keep them in the house if possible while the Confederate soldiers were busy outside preparing to make things interesting for the visitors when they came out.

Andrew Anderson tells a story about Russian Sam and Jack Hardin who went out to sink a boat called the *Breakers* to keep the Yankees from getting her, taking a sack of gunpowder with them to throw down in the bottom of the boat after starting a fire, but instead of throwing the gunpowder down the hold they threw a sack of sugar down, in their excitement, and waded ashore with the gunpowder, wondering why the boat didn't blow up. The enemy soon came and took her away. Jack Sands' fine sloop *Hannah* and another boat called *Elmer* were burned.

At the breakup of the war in 1865, the writer was attending school at the Hidalgo Seminary, when Dr. Merriman, father of the writer, called him to come at once and go with him to Col. Lovenskiold's home, where some important news had just came in by boat. In reply to what the news was, Mrs. Lovenskiold said, "The war is ended, General Lee has surrendered, and Abraham Lincoln has been assassinated."

That was enough, and away we went as fast as we could go to Dr. Merriman's hospital in the old home of Captain John Rabb[18] where Dr. Merriman announced the news to sick soldiers, many of them in the outhouses hardly able to get up, some of them suffering from diseases from their long service in the army.

An hour or so later found us on our way to Banquete, where Dr. Merriman had another hospital with sick soldiers. On the prairie about where Robstown is now located, we met Col. Lovenskiold

---

[18] The house, moved to Heritage Park, is known today as the Merriman-Bobys House.

with his two sisters-in-law, coming from Brownsville. Lovenskiold was in trouble, halted and surrounded by men who were ready to take his life. Dr. Merriman, who was surprised at what he saw, pleaded with the men — some of them he knew, probably Confederate soldiers he had doctored — to let the colonel go. They replied that they were turned loose without a dollar in the world, hundreds of miles from their homes and families that they had not heard from in many months. The doctor replied that they could take the colonel's money and let him go to Corpus Christi with the ladies. To this they agreed, and Col. Lovenskiold, who was a close friend of Dr. Merriman, was allowed to proceed on his way. Lovenskiold was Merriman's lawyer and Merriman was the colonel's family physician.

The whole country was in a state of chaos at the close of the war, generally the case with a defeated army turned loose. Might was right, some people seemed to think. Wagons with provisions coming from Brownsville and Matamoros were attacked by jayhawkers who, when resistance was made, shot some of the drivers. Even during the war, in 1863, Herman Meuly says Jayhawker Cox and his men came into Corpus Christi and took five thousand dollars' worth of merchandise out of his father's store on Chaparral Street, Mr. Windish reporting his father as a renegade.

Right after the close of the war a man named Scheuer, a good man, opened a store in the Staples Building, opposite Noakes,[19] when a man named Jim Garner, dangerous when drinking, asked for a pair of boots. He refused to pay for them and was about to ride away on his horse when Scheuer was called to the door, it is said, Mr. Scheuer telling the man he couldn't give him credit.[20] Garner pulled his gun and shot Scheuer through the heart. News of the murder spread quickly and a vigilance committee was organized at once, the people saying that it was high time something was done, and to get a rope, and they got one — about half a block long, so that everybody could get a pull at it. In a short time they found the

---

[19] 307 North Chaparral.
[20] Emanuel Scheuer and Jim Garner had served in W. S. Shaw's Confederate militia company. Muster rolls list Scheuer as a corporal and Garner as a private.

murderer and dragged him along to about·where the C.C. Hardware store is now located,[21] where they hung him to a tree, higher than Hayman, some said. The next morning his dad came and took the body down, saying that he had got a long stake-rope by the operation.

There were several regiments of U.S. troops sent to Corpus Christi at the close of the war, pitching their tents with Old Glory waving in the breezes on the bluff and on the beach. A company of Negro soldiers — a hundred men or more coming with them, did not remain long; some of them getting whisky, were very insulting, causing an uprising among the whites. For a while things looked bad like there was going to be bloodshed, and there would have been, had not the Negro troops been ordered away. Daddy Grant[22] took them off on his boat down to Point Isabel, it is said.

An office was opened at the Russell place, now the Royal Givens home, for Confederates to take the oath of allegiance to the United States. Some took the oath while others refused, saying they did not have to sign it.

After the war there was a good deal said about "carpetbaggers," but the term did not apply to many of the Northerners coming to Corpus Christi, the government officers and soldiers making many friends here. Military balls were given frequently, attended by some of the leading citizens and their families — North and South joining hands, resulting in several surprising marriages. Major James Downing married a daughter[23] of Major Blucher, the man who fired the first shot at Capt. Kittridge's flagship. Col. D. M. Layman married the widow Noessel (the Noessels were staunch Democrats)[24] and E. H. Wheeler, the sweet singer, another government official, married a daughter of Judge John S. McCampbell, a dyed-in-the-wool Democrat. Col. Nelson Plato was

---

[21] At 99 South Broadway.

[22] Capt. James Grant, a native of Halifax, Nova Scotia.

[23] Lt. James Downing married Mary Blucher, daughter of Felix and Maria von Blucher, on Nov. 16, 1867.

[24] Political divisions in Texas after the war were roughly this: Confederates and Southern patriots were Democrat and Yankees and Unionists and occupation officials were Republican.

elected mayor of the city. General Brown proved his goodness by taking the young ladies out riding in his fine carriage, while Mr. C. B. G. Drummond waltzed with the ladies at the dances, swinging them right and left in the quadrilles. Major Ira Evans, a friend of Judge James O. Luby, was a jolly good fellow. He is said to be living at Austin. Judge Barden was appointed district judge and Oceola Archer, district attorney. In those days colored men served on the juries with the whites and rode in carriages. Verily, this is a world of change.

Eli T. Merriman (1852-1941) (Plate 14) was born near Brownsville, the son of Dr. and Mrs. Eli T. Merriman. Dr. Merriman moved to Banquete and Eli was sent to school in Corpus Christi during the Civil War. At war's end, the family moved to Corpus Christi. After Dr. Merriman died in the yellow fever epidemic of 1867, Mrs. Merriman kept a boarding house on Mesquite Street. In 1870, Eli Merriman, then 18, went to work for the *Nueces Valley* newspaper. In 1877, he and William Maltby began publishing the *Corpus Christi Free Press*. When Maltby died, Merriman bought his half of the paper. In 1880, he married Ellen Robertson; they had three children. In 1883, Merriman, J. P. Caruthers and Ed Williams began the *Corpus Christi Caller*. After Caruthers and Williams left, Merriman continued as editor and publisher until 1912, when he sold the *Caller* to Henrietta M. King. Over his long tenure as editor, he was an advocate for railroads, a deepwater port, street improvements and development of a reliable water supply for Corpus Christi. He wrote about the history of Corpus Christi and sought to protect and preserve Old Bayview Cemetery. Interview dates for the Random Recollections segment by Marie Blucher were from Nov. 9, 1938 to Oct. 9, 1940. Reminiscences of the Civil War segment June 2, 1929. Eli T. Merriman died after a fall on Jan. 25, 1941, at the age of 88 years.

PLATES

Plate 1 - Robert Adams

When he was five years old in 1852, Robert Adams' family left England for Corpus Christi. He grew up to became a sheepherder and cattle rancher in Nueces County, which was later Jim Wells County.

NUECES VALLEY
LAND & EMIGRATION OFFICE,

3, Church Court, Clement's Lane, London.

For Sale:

300,000 ACRES OF LAND IN ONE SQUARE BLOCK.

THE HON. COL. H. L. KINNEY, the proprietor of the above extensive domain, having appointed the undersigned his sole agents for the disposal of the above lands to settlers and capitalists, they are authorized on his behalf to offer to Emigrants the following liberal terms:—

To ANY FAMILY OF GOOD REPUTE FOR HONESTY, industry, and perseverance, he will let them have ten cows on shares; he will sell them one hundred acres of land at six shillings per acre; also one yoke of oxen, and one horse; two shillings per acre to be paid to the agents in London, on execution of the contract,—and the balance for the land and stock to be paid in ten years, with interest annually; he will also give to each family one building lot in the town of Nueces. A reduced quantity of land may be had subject to arrangement.

IT MAY BE ASKED, WHY THIS LIBERALTY?—The proprietor is the owner of 12,000 head of horned cattle, 2,000 stock horses, mares, and mules, 10,000 sheep; and being resident on the estate, he is thus enabled to offer to emigrants advantages that no other man in the United States can command.

THESE HIGHLY PRODUCTIVE LANDS, being a dark deep loam, well adapted for all agricultural purposes, are beautifully situated on the bay of Corpus Christi, and the Nueces River, Western Texas, from which there is weekly communication by steam with Galveston, New Orleans, and other ports; and there being an extensive demand in the home districts, and for the northern markets, insures a ready cash sale for produce of every description.

CORPUS CHRISTI, situated in the vicinity of this property, is a town of considerable commercial activity, and being the chief mart for merchandize for the western districts of Texas and the Rio Grande country, is fast rising into importance: in fact, the natural position of this locality, having good roads, with extensive water facilities, cannot fail to command a large and extended commerce with the surrounding country in every direction, thus offering to the *agriculturist, the merchant, the trader, the mechanic, and the labourer*, a field of no ordinary character for the successful pursuit of their respective occupations.

THE SOIL AND CLIMATE of this region is unsurpassed,—two full crops of corn and other cereals in perfection, are secured annually. Irish and sweet potatoes, with all other roots and vegetables, make large returns; the peach, the vine, and other fruit trees thrive luxuriantly.

THERE IS AN ABUNDANT and never-failing supply of water; TIMBER of the finest quality for all useful and ornamental purposes; *and three-fourths of the land being gently undulating prairie*, can be made immediately available for the plough, thus effecting a saving of twenty dollars per acre in clearing, an outlay that must be submitted to by settlers in most other parts of the Union.

THIS SECTION OF THE COUNTRY, justly described "the FAIREST REGION OF AMERICA," is singularly free from swamps and stagnant water; there being no fogs or damp air, fever, ague, and other epidemies, are unknown; and no country in the world offers such advantages for the breeding of stock, the range of pasture being almost unlimited. There is perpetual verdure and no provision is necessary for the keep of cattle during the winter; it, therefore, we presume, offers incomparable advantages to all those in search of a HAPPY HOME, with the certainty of speedily acquiring independence for themselves and families.

Cotton of the finest staple, also sugar and tobacco, are cultivated to great perfection without the aid of slaves; the country being so healthy, the unacclimated perform field labour at all seasons without inconvenience. Range of the thermometer, 35 to 85.

IN THE RISING TOWN OF NUECES, situated on the property of Col. Kinney, and on his adjoining lands, there are already located upwards of a thousand individuals; therefore the emigrant will at once enjoy the benefit of association with a thrifty, active, and experienced population.

Plate 2 - Kinney's handbill

Henry Kinney distributed pamphlets, or handbills, in England and Scotland offering land for sale in the Nueces Valley area of South Texas.

Plate 3 - William Adams

William Adams arrived in Corpus Christi when he was six with his family from England, attracted to Texas by Henry Kinney's land sales. With his brother Robert, he became a rancher and helped organize Jim Wells County in 1912.

Plate 4 - Battle of Corpus Christi

Thomas Noakes' sketch of the battle of Corpus Christi when Union forces from blockading ships landed on North Beach, then bombarded Corpus Christi in August 1862.

Plate 5 - Andrew Anderson

Andrew Anderson's father, John Anderson, a ship captain, carried supplies from New Orleans to Corpus Christi for Zachary Taylor's army, then moved his family to Corpus Christi. Capt. Andrew Anderson became a bay pilot and owned the schooner *Flour Bluff* and the pleasure boat Japonica.

Plate 6 – The Ohler Building

This is perhaps the oldest known photo of Corpus Christi, believed to be the Ohler building, possibly taken in the early 1850s. The back of the photo, at the Corpus Christi Central Library, identifies it as a landmark structure built on the waterfront in 1848. From other sources, including R. Hollub's 1874 sketch of the waterfront, it appears to be the Ohler building. Andrew Anderson, who lived next door, remembered the Ohler family living upstairs and operating a store below.

Plate 7 - The Anderson windmill

Capt. John Anderson built a windmill next to the Anderson home on Water Street in 1874. The windmill powered a grist wheel to grind salt and a saw to cut firewood.

Plate 8 - Schooner *Flour Bluff*

The schooner was built in 1860 by Captain John Anderson, rebuilt in 1879 and rebuilt again in 1900. The *Flour Bluff* was later owned by Capt. Andrew Anderson. It was destroyed by the hurricane of 1919.

Plate 9 - Edey & Kirsten

This major wool-buying firm was located on Lawrence Street opposite the
St. James Hotel. Note the sheep or "borrego" on the roof.

Plate 10 - Anna Moore Schwien

Anna's mother Malvina, a slave, arrived in Corpus Christi in 1849. Anna Moore, born as a slave in 1856, became a teacher and married a German immigrant named Schweine.

Plate 11 - Magnolia Mansion

Martha Rabb, called the cattle queen of Texas, built a mansion on Broadway in Corpus Christi. After Mrs. Rabb remarried and moved to Austin, it was bought by Mifflin Kenedy for his son John G. Kenedy.

Plate 12 - Woessner's wool store

John Woessner was one of the principal wool dealers in Corpus Christi. His store, wool warehouse, and home was on Chaparral at Starr.

Plate 13 - Centennial House

Anna Moore Schwien said Forbes Britton's house, known as Centennial House today, was being built on the bluff when her mother, Malvina, arrived in Corpus Christi on Jan. 1, 1849. This photo is from the 1930s.

Plate 14 - Eli Merriman

The son of a doctor, Eli Merriman began his newspaper career in 1870, working for the *Nueces Valley*, and in 1883 was one of three founders of the *Corpus Christi Caller*. He served as editor of the paper until 1912.

Central Wharf, Corpus Christi, Tex.

Plate 15 - Central Wharf

A furious controversy split Corpus Christi in the 1870s after several merchants gained monopoly control of the Central Wharf. They were opposed by a faction called the anti-monopoly group. This photograph of Central Wharf is from the early 1900s.

Plate 16 - Alta Vista Hotel

E. H. Ropes, land speculator and venture capitalist, built the Alta Vista Hotel at Three Mile Point on today's Ocean Drive. The Ropes-inspired boom collapsed in a money panic in 1893. The old hotel burned in 1927.

Plate 17 - E. H. Caldwell

The son of a Presbyterian pastor, Edward Harvey Caldwell came to Corpus Christi in 1872. He worked as a clerk for Doddridge, Lott & Davis, wool merchants, tried sheep ranching then entered the hardware business.

Plate 18 - E. H. Caldwell's Hardware Store

In 1902, wagonloads of well casing pipe leave Chaparral Street for King Ranch. Men stand in the doorways of two firms connected with supplying artesian well equipment — E.H. Caldwell's Hardware and Randolph Robertson's Dempster Well Machinery. Caldwell's Hardware supplied ranchers with everything from guns to barbed wire to windmills.

Plate 19 - Doddridge Bank

Perry Doddridge and Allen M. Davis, who purchased the wool business
of Edey & Kirsteen in 1868, opened the first bank in Corpus Christi in
1871. The Doddridge Bank was on the east side of Chaparral across from
the St. James Hotel. This photograph is from the 1890s.

Plate 20 - Perry Doddridge

Doddridge was engaged in the Mexican trade at Roma and Mier before he moved to Corpus Christi, became a wool merchant and opened the town's first bank, with Allen M. Davis.

Plate 21 - The Hollub Courthouse

Nueces County's second courthouse, built in 1875, was designed by Major Rudolph Hollub, a former officer in the Austrian army who was an aide to Gen. U.S. Grant in the Civil War. He came to Corpus Christi as an engineer in building the Tex-Mex Railroad.

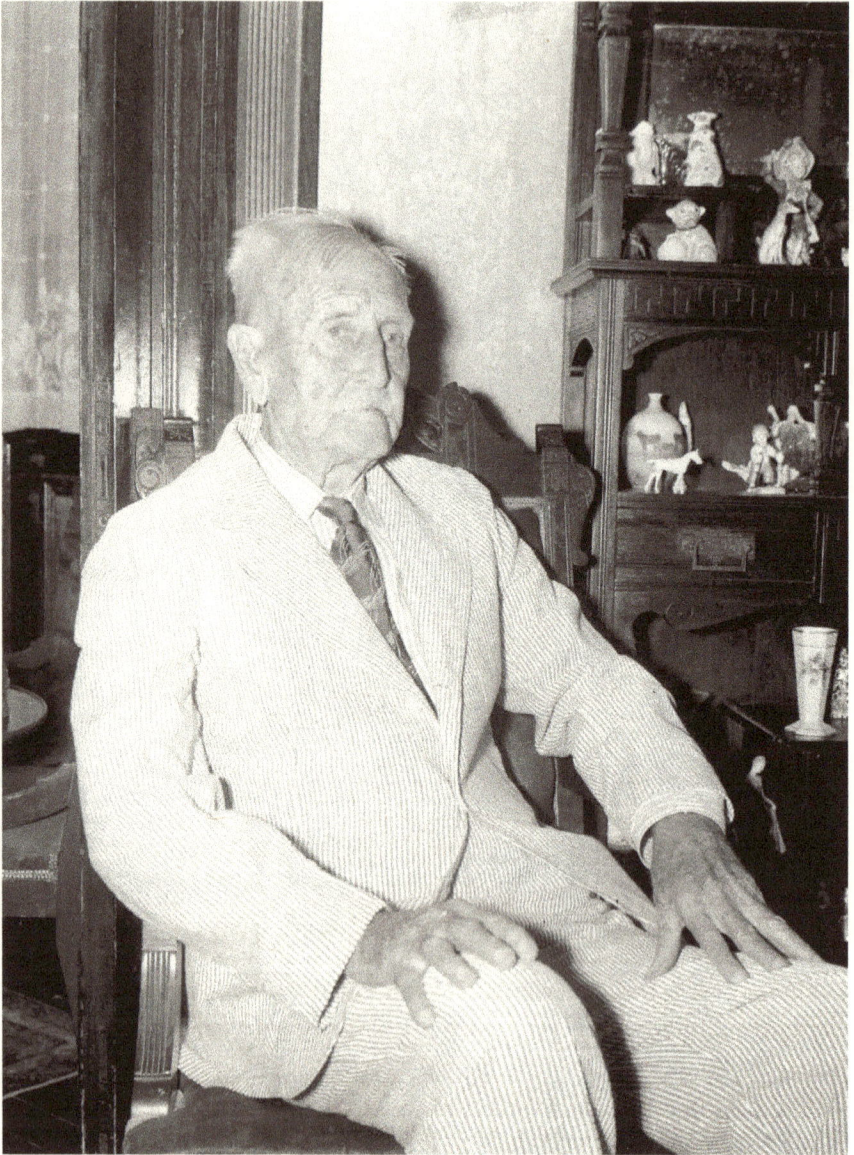

Plate 22 - W. S. Rankin

William S. (Bill) Rankin, whose parents moved from Scotland to Corpus
Christi in 1853, began work as a painter, later owned a paint store, then
entered the retail grocery business.

Plate 23 - Rankin's Grocery

W. S. (Bill) Rankin operated a retail grocery business in the 1880s on the ground floor of the McCampbell Building, at Mesquite and Peoples, across from the Market Hall. The upstairs was occupied by the law firm of John McCampbell and John S. Givens.

Plate 24 - Thomas John Noakes (a self-portrait)

Noakes left his home at Sussex, England, in 1845 as a young man and came to Texas. He settled at Nuecestown, where he farmed and later built a store, which was burned during a bandit raid in 1875.

Plate 25 - Market Hall

Built by two businessmen in 1871, Market Hall served as the city's municipal building, with city offices and a civic meeting place upstairs, quarters for volunteer firemen, and stalls for butchers and vegetable vendors on the first floor.

Plate 26 - Ruth Dodson

Ruth Dodson, the daughter of Milton and Susan Dodson, was born on the Perdido Ranch, the former ranch of Martin Culver. One of her neighbors was Henry A. Gilpin.

Plate 27 - Martin Culver

Culver learned the cattle business on his uncle's ranch at Oakville. He bought Rancho Perdido (the Lost Ranch) on Penitas Creek after the Civil War. Culver, a free-range cattleman, drove huge herds up the trail to Kansas.

Plate 28 - Martin Culver ranch house

Milton Dodson, Ruth Dodson's father, is sitting on the porch of the Rancho Perdido ranch house, built by Martin S. Culver in 1871 three miles southwest of Casa Blanca, in today's Jim Wells County.

Plate 29 - Henry Addington Gilpin (photo of bas relief)

Gilpin landed trade goods at Corpus Christi in 1829, became a partner of Belden & Mann in the 1840s, was chief justice of Nueces County, then retired to his Penitas Ranch, next door to Milton Dodson's ranch.

Plate 30 - J. Frank Dobie

Dobie was born and raised on his father's ranch in Live Oak County. His early life on the ranch became the bedrock for his works. Dobie's books include "A Vaquero of the Brush Country," "Coronado's Children," "The Longhorns," "The Mustangs," "The Voice of the Coyote," and many others.

Plate 31 - James M. (Jim) Dobie

J. Frank Dobie's uncle, his father's brother, was the big cattle rancher in the Dobie family. In 1886, he and Dobie's father became partners in the Live Oak County ranch on Ramirenia Creek where the famous Texas writer was born.

Plate 32 - Taft Visit

President William Howard Taft came to South Texas in October 1909 to visit his half-brother at the Taft Ranch. He visited Corpus Christi on Oct. 22 and addressed a large crowd gathered on the side of the bluff, later named Spohn Park. Roy Terrell was among the schoolchildren assembled to listen to the president's speech.

Plate 33 - Cal Allen

Roy Terrell's mother's brother, Calvin J. Allen, founded the community known as Calallen.

Plate 34 - Barrileros

Roy Terrell remembered when water carriers known as "barrileros" traveled down the streets selling water at 25 cents a barrel. In the early days, they filled their barrels from the Nueces River. After the city built a pipeline to the river at Calallen, the barrileros filled their barrels at one of the city's standpipes. This one was at Mestina and Sam Rankin streets.

Plate 35 – Louis Rawalt

Louis Rawalt rolls along a barrel of tar salvaged on a Padre Island beach while his three-year-old son Charlie follows behind.

CHAPTER 6

E. H. CALDWELL
CROSSING THE REEF

I had been in this country only six months when I had an experience crossing the reef which I shall never forget. It was in 1872 when I was only 21 years old.

Returning from a trip to Refugio I lost my bearings. There were no roads. You went across country, which was covered with prickly pear, mesquite and chaparral, with nothing more than motts of trees by which to get your directions. I lost my way to the extent that, instead of reaching the bay at the crossing, I reached it somewhere in the vicinity of White Point. I could see Corpus Christi across the water, and so made my way along the shore until I reached the crossing. But on account of having to go around so many gullies that had washed in the cliffs along the bay shore, it was getting dark when I got to where Portland is now.

I was a little nervous, having heard tales about the murder of a white man by Mexicans in this exact vicinity. Just as I went down the slope to the water I caught a glimpse of two figures on horseback some distance in the rear. My heart nearly stopped beating. I was sure they were Mexicans and that my life was in danger.

I was on a good horse and made my way as quickly as I could through the shallow water of the bay, following the line of stakes that marked the course of the crossing. But the men seemed to be gaining on me. Finally I removed my boots, hung them on the saddle, and let myself down into the water. I carefully worked my horse to a point deep enough for me to crouch under the water, with only my head showing, tied my horse to a stake, and moved a little farther away. All this time I could dimly see the two men coming closer and closer to me. To say that I was frightened was putting it mildly, for I felt that my chances of not being discovered were slim indeed.

Very soon the two men reached my vicinity. To my intense relief, they didn't see me, and passed on without molesting either myself or my horse. As soon as I felt they were out of hearing I made my way to my horse and finished my journey home. My feet were badly cut by oyster shells and the immersion in the cold water caused chills to set in. I was in bed for two weeks following this eventful crossing of the reef.

In those times, it was not unusual sight to see ox-carts reaching from way up on Leopard Street down the bluff to Chaparral Street and up Chaparral as far as the Wrather place in the 900 block.

The principal buyers of wool and hides were Doddridge, Lott & Davis, Ed Buckley, Frank & Weil, D. Hirsch, John Woessner (Plate 12), and Norwick Gussett. At the establishments of these men the ox-carts would unload wool, hides, goat skins and other wares, and would take on a return cargo of supplies from stores owned by these and others, including Julius Henry the merchant. The hides were stored in warehouses along the bay.

Uriah Lott and his partner later had a great deal of business with mule teams to Chihuahua, Mexico, using special mule-team wagons. However, these did not put the ox-carts out of business. The railroads did that by cutting off the Mexican trade, leaving Corpus Christi only what could be secured from the points down below Laredo.

At the rear of Doddridge, Lott & Davis's office, corner of Chaparral and Lawrence streets, their warehouse extended clear back to Water Street. In 1872, right in this vicinity — back of the Staples Building and extending into the bay — was Staples' Wharf, so-called because Mr. Staples[1] landed his lumber there for his lumberyard on Water Street.

I was working for Doddridge, Lott & Davis and recall the destruction of this wharf in the storm of 1873.[2] I stood on Water Street and watched that wharf going up and down on the heaving waters. This storm was worse in Corpus Christi than that of 1875, which did so much damage at Indianola. Staples Wharf was not rebuilt, as Central Wharf had been built by this time (Plate 15).

The banking firm of Doddridge & Company (Plate 19), through the Central Wharf & Warehouse Company, assisted in financing the Morris & Cummings channel for deep water, and had exclusive right to collect tolls at the Central Wharf. No steamers could come to Corpus Christi through this channel without using that wharf. Norwick Gussett, merchant, who owned some light-draft schooners, built a warehouse and wharf on North Beach, near where the Breakers Hotel is now.[3] Bringing his freight in these boats and docking at his own wharf, he offered lively competition to the Doddridge company.

Gussett's warehouse later became Tom Beynon's livery stable on North Tancahua Street. It had been built originally in the early 1870s (torn down in April 1940 to make room for a parking lot for the Piggly-Wiggly store).

During the period between 1875 and 1884, I lived on the Borjas Ranch where my brothers — George, Willie and Walter — and I carried on a ranching enterprise. Although nothing now remains to show where the ranch house was, it was well known in those days as one of the many hospitable establishments of this frontier section.

---

[1] Wayman N. (W.N.) Staples was the Corpus Christi merchant. His brother, William W. Staples, owned a ranch in Live Oak County. Both came from Alabama in the 1850s.

[2] Mr. Caldwell may have had his dates confused. A storm on Sept. 5, 1874 caused considerable damage along the bayfront in downtown Corpus Christi; there was no such hurricane that hit the city in 1873.

[3] 3614 Hamilton Road.

About halfway between Corpus Christi and Laredo, the Borjas was about 13 miles from Benavides and about seven miles from Realitos. It was off the railroad but was on the main route crossing this portion of the state toward the Mexican border.

The house, built of ciar rock — the same material which forms caliche when pulverized — consisted of a reception room at one end, which also served as a storeroom for supplies to be sold, and at the other end a room used as a store. Over the former, the main room of the house, was built a second-story room used for sleeping purposes, which was fitted out to serve as a fort in an emergency. Each wall was built with port-holes, but these were concealed by being plastered over on the outside. If at any time they had to be used, the plaster could quickly be punched away from the inside with a gun.

Having friends in Laredo and Corpus Christi, as well as along the route, we had a great deal of company. Many people traveled back and forth and they always made it a point to stop. There were seldom as many as three or four days between the visits of people who would stop and spend the night with us. There was a constant stream of visitors. We never thought of charging a cent for bed or food, and neither did they expect to pay. That was the custom on the frontier. Anyone who wanted to could come and stay. They were gladly given free water, grass and meals, and there was no bill to pay.

The pleasure of these overnight stops was mutual. The more people we had on the ranch, the better protected we were. We didn't worry about the Mexican families who had their little ranches there. They were friendly and, in the main, good citizens. But this was a frontier section almost as much as down on the Rio Grande. There were no fences to stop the raiding parties which, consisting of from two to 50 people, sometimes came over from across the river to attack a store or any settlement they took a notion to. Protection from the lawless was a feature of that day and time.

In addition to this aspect of having overnight visitors on the ranch, we derived much pleasure from hearing news of the outside world brought to us by these travelers, news which we wouldn't get otherwise. Anecdotes and stories enlivened the evenings and helped to lift the loneliness that settled on this remote spot as soon as the guests traveled on.

The spirit of hospitality exhibited at this ranch was not unique, but was typical of the hospitality existing all over this part of the country. We never thought of the cost of it, as we felt repaid by the company and the protection. We were glad to entertain anybody and everybody who came, and they, in turn, were glad to be entertained, giving in return protection and the news of the world as they knew it.

Our most frequent guests were traveling salesmen. These men always had a fund of anecdotes and humorous news. Some were expert cooks who would "dish up" something new occasionally. You see, in those days, there were no hotels at which to stop and eat, and many people carried food along and cooked it wherever they could stop to do so.

The salesmen usually traveled by hack or ambulance, although a few had a pair of horses and a buggy or hack of their own. Each salesman was usually accompanied by a helper. They handled everything that went to make up the commerce between Texas and Mexico. Among the best-known merchandise firms represented were Zuberier & Behan and Rice, Born & Company, both of New Orleans.

Among occasional guests at the ranch were other ranchmen. All the ranchmen of this section felt free to enjoy our hospitality. Visitors of another type were sometimes entertained unawares. Our being on a frontier explains the presence of a great many criminals drifting along through this country, men who had come from the states beyond Texas desiring to be near the border where they could get quickly over into Mexico. One man who stayed overnight with us was a lame man who used a crutch. As usual, no questions were asked, no names given, no personal conversation indulged in. It sufficed that he was a traveler, and we gave him haven for the night. It never occurred to me that he was a man I had known well back in Tennessee many years before. But such proved later to be the case. He had killed an especial friend of mine in Tennessee, had escaped, and was fleeing to Mexico.

While we made it a practice never to charge for accomodations at the ranch, there was a single exception to this custom on our part. A party of several men arrived just about dusk in the afternoon and asked to stay the night. We didn't like their looks, and so referred the matter to the partner who was cook for that week (my brother George). He first said, "No, I don't want them. I don't like their looks. They are not our sort."

But it was getting dark and it was 15 miles distant to any other place. We told my brother to handle it any way he thought best. And so he said, "All right. I'll let them stay. But I'll make them pay for it." Next morning the head of the party began thanking us for the hospitality and we referred him to the cook. He began to thank the cook, who said, "That's all right. Your bill is five dollars."

"Why," the man replied. "We understood that you never make any charge against anybody."

"Yes, that is a fact. But we are making an exception this time."

"Why?" inquired the visitor.

"Well, because you are not our sort," answered the cook. "Your bill is five dollars."

The bill was paid, but these particular visitors never asked for accommodations at our ranch again.

During the lulls between visitors, one became very lonesome. While these intervals were short, I recall one instance in which 45 days passed by without my seeing any person who could speak English.

Another time, there was a lull just before Christmas. By the time Christmas Day came, I was so lonely that when there arrived a young man who had aroused my severest resentment, almost hate, a few years before, I actually asked him to stop and visit with me for a while. The Christmas spirit, the lonesomeness, and the passing of time, all contributed to my cordiality, and I felt really glad to see the boy.

After all, the cause of my resentment was trivial in itself, just one of those little incidents which build up antagonisms between human beings that sometime last a lifetime. This young man and his brothers had merely made fun of me, and I hated them for it. They considered me a tenderfoot a few years before, because I had just arrived in Texas. When a little pony I had hopped on to go a short distance threw me off, into the wet grass, these boys had laughed and hooted at me so loudly that after that I had nothing to do with them.

On one occasion the Collector of Customs was a visitor at the ranch, as was his practice when he made his rounds through the district. There were so many in his party the ranch house could not accommodate them and they camped for the night down by the water. The collector called his deputy and told him to mix up a drink for one of his hosts. The deputy said, "Why, he never drinks anything. I know him well." The Collector replied, "You don't know anything about how to offer a man a drink. You go mix him up a stiff toddy, and stick it under his nose, and see what he'll do about it." And it worked.

The Borjas ranch house no longer stands. The lands are divided between livestock raising and oil wells. The ranch no longer exists as it did then. The days of frontier dangers are past. But the hospitality extended to visitors at the Borjas and at other ranches of the Southwest contributed its part to the life of that day and time.

———

The raid on Noakes' store in 1875, referred to in some accounts as having occurred in April, took place on March 26th. Certain vivid memories place the date unmistakably in my mind. I had just come out to the Borjas Ranch, which was 27 miles west of San Diego on the road to Laredo. I had just bought some sheep on Saturday, March 27th, and had just moved in with them to Borjas on Saturday night, when three men came riding up to where I was in camp.

The captain was riding a horse that I recognized as belonging to George Reynolds, who was a prominent sheep man and owner of the Ventana Ranch. I knew then that these men were robbers and thieves and suspected that a gang of raiders were passing with a bunch of stolen horses. The three rode up to me at my campfire. They asked me to show them where the water was — they wanted water. As I could hear horses splashing and men shouting at them in the dark, I knew that was only an excuse. They wanted to get me out and then they would get the ammunition and the guns. I refused to go with them. They rode off and I turned to my Mexican shepherd and asked him if he knew how to shoot. He replied that he did.

"Will you shoot if I tell you to?" I asked him.

"*Si, senor.*"

"Do you know what those men were?"

"*Si, son ladrones*" (they are robbers).

"Will you shoot to kill if I tell you to?"

"*Si.*"

I went into the jacal and got my rifle and pistol, which I didn't have on me at the time. I was in the act of showing the Mexican how to load his gun (he would shoot, but not load his gun) when the men again rode upon us in the dark before I knew what was happening. I automatically rose up with the gun in my hand, loaded and cocked, pointed right at the captain's heart. It was purely accidental.

The captain of the band again wanted me to show him water. We had quite an argument in Spanish. They couldn't do anything because I had the captain at my mercy. It was not bravery on my part. I realized I had the drop. They rode off and I didn't lose a minute's time leaving the camp. The Mexican and I got off our blankets and ran off into the chaparral to spend the night. That was my first night as a sheep man — March 27, 1875.

It was not until Sunday morning when Sidney Borden and his company of men[4] arrived at Borjas that I knew that the gang of the night before were the Mexican raiders who, after burning Noakes' store near Corpus Christi on Good Friday, had covered the distance of 85 miles in 24 hours.

With respect to this raid of March 26, 1875, and the pursuit of the raiders, I wish to state the following, to keep the record clear. The party of men from Corpus Christi who went out to attack the Mexican raiders comprised the following: John B. Dunn, James

---

[4] Sidney Borden, founder of Sharpsburg, was captured by the bandits. After he was freed, he raised a posse to go after the bandits.

Dunn and Matt Dunn, three brothers who were cousins of Pat and Lawrence, also cousins of John Dunn; Pat and Lawrence Dunn, brothers, cousins of the three listed above and cousins of John; John Dunn, a cousin of the Dunns listed above; George Dunn, son of Joe "Vegetable" Dunn, not related to the other Dunns listed here;[5] Washington Mussett, Bass Burriss, George W. Swank, Clem Vetters, Pat Whelan, Jesus Seguira.

To pursue the raiders after they left the vicinity of Corpus Christi, three companies were made up. One company started out on the theory that the raiders were heading north to San Antonio. One company, of which Sidney Borden was captain, struck out toward Laredo. The third started out toward Santa Gertrudis thinking the raiders would take a short cut to the Rio Grande.

Sidney Borden's company finally got the trail and passed my house at the Borjas Ranch Sunday morning, the 28th. But they were nearly 12 hours behind the raiders. I told them they could not possibly overtake the raiders before they could get to the Rio Grande and over into Mexico. When the Borden party reached the border they found that the raiders had, indeed, crossed the river and were safe from their pursuers.

Marion Garner, who was a member of Sidney Borden's company, has left an account of the raid, from which most of the above was corroborated.

The Star Rifles were not in existence at the time of the raid. I just want to get this point cleared up, which has been asserted by some saying that the Star Rifles went out on the steamer at the end of the wharf for protection, as many citizens did. This fine group was organized following the raid, and must have been confused with some other organization existing earlier.

---

[5] Five Irish-born Dunn brothers had large families and the names of their sons were duplicated with John, Matt, Thomas, Peter, etc. People learned to distinguish between them by nicknames, such as "Red John" Dunn rather than plain John Dunn. The Dunns involved in chasing the Nuecestown raiders were brothers and cousins.

Along about 1884 or 1885, soon after I had returned to Corpus Christi from the Borjas Ranch, there was a lot of excitement here about smallpox. There was no epidemic, but there were a few cases among the Mexicans. The health authorities proposed segregating them out along Nueces Bay, back of Last Street, in the pest house, which was maintained by the health service of Corpus Christi for cases of communicable disease.

The Mexicans objected to this proposal. They armed themselves and were going to fight. A certain Mexican, prominent on the hill, who had a big following, was the head of the opposition to the plan for segregation of the smallpox cases.

I had guns for sale and this man wanted to get about $500 worth. I tried to bluff him out of it by asking for cash for the purchase. He surprised me by bringing a bag with the $500. I told him to wait a little while and went to consult G. R. Scott, lawyer, to see if it was all right for me to let him have the firearms. Mr. Scott advised against it. I returned and told the man that I couldn't let him have the guns, even for cash. He departed in great indignation, but a riot was averted — and an epidemic was averted as well, for the health authorities, backed by Elias Mussett, city marshal, succeeded in transferring the sick Mexicans to the pest house.

Preventive efforts against epidemics in those early days included patrolling the borders of the town to see that people from Brownsville and Laredo in particular, and elsewhere as well, did not come in with the smallpox or yellow fever. Different people assisted in this patrol work. I served two or three times. They went out, especially at night, although some lookouts were on duty all the time. There was a yellow fever scare here about 1887.

Among the names that come to mind quickly when I think of the early citizens of this city are the following:

Father O'Reilly.[6] He was here before I came in 1872. He taught Catholic children in a shell concrete building on Mesquite Street, located in the present Spohn Park and facing east. Rev. Horton, a Methodist minister,[7] and Rev. Perham,[8] a Methodist minister, also

---

[6] Father Bernard O'Reilly.
[7] Rev. H. J. Horton.

taught private school. Priours, John M., and Julian. George Hobbs, who had a store west of Jordts present home on Antelope. J. A. Ware, a lawyer. Pat McDonough, county clerk.

Judge Pryor Lea, grandfather of Mrs. W. H. Caldwell (Miss Janie Dill), spent a fortune trying to get deep water, especially from Aransas Pass (channel) to Rockport. He worked in a print shop. Made artificial stone. John M. Moore also "went broke" trying to get deep water. The boiler of his dredge boat was to be seen for many years at the edge of the bay. It gradually disappeared from sight.

W. L. Rogers built a home on Chaparral Street in 1871. It burned down and he started a new home the next day. This house is still standing, opposite the SAMSCO building,[9] facing east. Rogers was sheriff of Nueces County at one time. During one of the Indian raids, he was left for dead, but survived.[10]

Rev. Homer S. Thrall, Methodist minister in Corpus Christi and Texas historian.

The Dunn family. There were five original brothers (no effort is made to give the names in consecutive order) as follows: Pat, father of Lawrence and Tom; Thomas, father of Pat, Thomas B. and Lawrence; Peter, father of Matt and Joe; John, father of Christopher, Nick, Joe, Pat, Matt, Mike, Lawrence and John (eight sons); Matthew, father of John B., Matt and James. There were three John Dunns, not seven, as some have thought; they were John, the old pioneer; his son John, born in Corpus Christi and still living in 1939; and his nephew, John B., also still living in 1939.

"Vegetable" Dunn. Joe Dunn, who had a son named George, was not related to the Dunns mentioned above.

The Whelan family. The father's name is not recalled. His sons were Pat, Tom, and John. William Ohler. He owned property in the

---

[8] Rev. J. P. Perham.

[9] It was located on South Chaparral across from Shook's Garage today. It was torn down in 1941.

[10] Rogers survived the massacre of a wagon train at Arroyo Colorado on the border at the start of the Mexican War. The killers were identified as Mexican bandits.

city, and later moved to North Beach Cedars. Grant family. William, Ed M., and John.

S. G. Miller.[11] He built a college at Lagarto. Did not live in Corpus Christi.

J. O. Luby, county judge of Duval County for many years.

Forbes Britton owned the Britton Ranch, some six miles or more southwest of Corpus Christi, living part of the time there and the remainder of the time in the city in the building at 411 North Broadway, known as the Bryden-Evans home (Plate 13).[12] Britton Motts were on the Britton Ranch, owned later by G. A. Rabb and possibly William Robertson.

Britton was the father of E. J. Davis's wife. Davis, governor of Texas at one time, built, owned and occupied the property at 715 North Broadway and sold the same to Norwick Gussett, who added to the building and lived in it until his death. The house was moved to 815 North Tancahua in 1937 to make room for the new post office.

James Barnard, father of Frank Barnard and father-in-law of Mary Bryden Barnard, figures in a humorous incident that occurred during the bombardment of this city in August 1862. Suffering from a desperate case of rheumatism, he was upstairs in the Gussett Building, lying on a cot, when a shell or cannonball shot through the east wall of the room. He heard the crash and was relieved of his rheumatism so completely that within the next few minutes he was far distant from his cot. In 1895, when I rented that store building for a merchandising business, the hole was still to be seen.

Mr. John Dix was a federal sympathizer. It is said that he had a secret understanding with the federals, whereby his hanging out a light at his home saved it from bombardment. This house later became the Seaside Hotel. It stood on Water Street, at the rear of the present Royal Givens' home (corner of North Chaparral and Taylor streets). Miss Mary Russell lived in the latter house, which

---

[11] S. G. (Sylvanus Gerard) Miller owned the Miller Ranch and operated a ferry on the Nueces River. Much of what comprised the Miller Ranch is under Lake Corpus Christi today.

[12] It is still on the original site, known as the Centennial House today.

was known as the Mary Russell house then. Mr. Dix was an elder in the Presbyterian Church here. He died before I came to Corpus Christi in 1872. His son, Capt. John J. Dix, lived several blocks north of his father in the house later known as the Welch home. This house was destroyed in the 1919 storm. Fannie Dix, daughter of Capt. John J. Dix, was a popular society girl. DeRyee owned the Seaside Hotel property at one time. He built a breakwater out of rocks brought from Laguna Madre by Capt. Will Anderson in his boat.

The Presbyterian Society, out of which grew the Presbyterian Church of Corpus Christi, was organized in 1866 in the three-gabled house at the southern end of South Broadway. It was known as the Hampton place, after Mr. and Mrs. Wade Hampton, who lived there. Mrs. Hampton was Lula Rabb, daughter of John Rabb, who built the house. Eli Merriman and Willie Rankin agree that it was probably built between 1847 and 1854. During the Civil War it was occupied by Eli Merriman's father as a hospital.[13]

Captain James Downing and Captain E. H. Wheeler were officers of the federal troops, who married Corpus Christi girls and remained here after their comrades had returned to the North. Capt. Downing married Mary Felicia von Blucher and Capt. Wheeler married Sarah Elizabeth McCampbell.

Norwick Gussett's first store was where Jordt-Allen was later (Allen Furniture Company now).[14] The second location was where the Texas Building is now, corner of Chaparral and Peoples streets. The third location was in the Shaw Building, now the Jones Building, corner of Chaparral and Schatzell. When Mr. Gussett came to Corpus Christi and opened a store in 1866, he bought from E. J. Davis his home at 715 North Broadway, including two lots, one fronting east on North Broadway, and one in the rear facing west; also four other lots north of the Davis home in the same block, from Levi Jones.

---

[13] The house was moved to Heritage Park; it is known today as the Merriman-Bobys House.

[14] 418 North Chaparral.

John Wade, later at Casa Blanca, owned the other six lots south of the Gussett home. The home on the front lots was owned and occupied by Mr. and Mrs. A. M. Davis during their life in this city. The house was removed to make room for the new post office building.

In the same vicinity Mr. Gocher, in 1872, operated a windmill; it was somewhere near the present homes of Horatio Gussett and Mrs. E. Morris, at Buffalo and North Broadway. It was elevated on a base of shell, sand and lime concrete and was used to grind grain for food for man and beast.

On North Broadway there was also a lighthouse, built by the government. This was north of the windmill, near the edge of the bluff and about east of the Congregational Church (colored), where the home of E. T. Merriman stands at 811 North Broadway.

John Anderson, father of John Jr., Andrew and William, owned and operated another windmill, located on Lot 4, Block 5, Beach. One of its chief uses was also to grind up salt during and after the Civil War,[15] the salt being brought up from the Laguna Madre and adjoining lakes by boats. For a good while this salt was the only supply the city had. The Anderson windmill may have been the first to use "ball bearings," as the upper part, facing the wind, was mounted on 12 cannonballs to facilitate moving the mill to face the prevailing or shifting direction of the winds.

"The Cedars" was the name given to a dense mott of these trees on the other side of the bayou. North Beach formerly was just like a prairie, with no trees at all. Someone planted salt cedars out there and they grew well and spread. In the vicinity of the Ohler home (on North Beach) there were no other trees nearby (nor any other houses), although there were many cedars between there and town.

Horace Taylor was postmaster of Corpus Christi from about 1872 to sometime in 1875, when he died. The post office at that time was in a little brick house facing west on Mesquite Street, at a point in the 200 block opposite the cannon now mounted in Spohn

---

[15] Capt. John Anderson did not build the windmill on Water Street until nine years after the war, in 1874.

150

Park. This would be just south of the Ford Agency display rooms. The bricks for the post office were made in Corpus Christi.

Mr. Louis de Planque's home was on the corner where the Ford agency is now (corner of Mesquite and William) with his photograph studio east of the home.

The public school building, incomplete in 1876, was at the same location as the Northside Junior High School is now. It was the same two-story frame building as was used until the present brick building was erected. They were building it in July 1876. I recall it well, because on July 4th of that year, during the 1776-1876 Fourth of July celebration, I sat in one of the windows to witness the celebration. This was the eventful day on which Stanley Welch's arm got shot off. He was firing a cannon, and it backfired. This occurred about where Mrs. Morris now lives, North Broadway and Buffalo streets.

When I came here in 1872 there was no organized state public school. Where the First Methodist Church now stands[16] there was a two-story frame building which housed a temperance organization upstairs and a private school downstairs.

Major Hollub[17] designed the second courthouse (Plate 21), which was known as the Hollub courthouse. He was the supervising engineer.

Perry Doddridge (Plate 20) was in business with a number of different persons at different times. The first firm name was Doddridge, Lott & Davis, bankers. Mr. Lott left the company to engage in building a railroad, and the firm became known as Doddridge & Davis; they were not only bankers, but also buyers and shippers of wool and hides. The third form of the firm was P. Doddridge & Co.

One of the most important things for this country was the finding and development of artesian wells and water in October 1899.

---

[16] Mesquite at the corner of Mann.

[17] Rudolph Hollub, a former officer in the Austrian army, was an aide to Gen. U.S. Grant in the Civil War. He came to Corpus Christi as an engineer in building what became the Tex-Mex Railroad.

J. T. James owned the St. James Hotel, selling it later to W. L. Rogers. Mr. James was a stockman on Mustang Island, where he lived and had his cattle.

The John Woessner two-story frame building (Plate 12) facing west on North Chaparral, now No. 622, was used for dances, roller skating, and other entertainments upstairs, and the first floor for various purposes. W. S. Rankin recalls attending dances there.

The Crescent Hotel was the correct name, in 1880, for what is generally remembered as the Steen Hotel. The latter name dates from about 1883.

William Cannon, a constable, owned and lived in the concrete dwelling on the corner of Mesquite and Starr streets (now Taylor Brothers store). He sold the property to Mrs. Sidbury, who dismantled the house and built her two-story residence there.

Captain S. T. Foster occupied the present Jordt house in 1880. Mrs. Mary Webster occupied it between 1883 and 1887 (at the corner of Antelope and North Carancahua).

Andrew and Peter Baldeschwiler were carpenters. Miss Teresa was their sister. Andrew claimed to be the first white child born in Corpus Christi, but this claim was disputed by Lee Riggs.

The lighthouse on the edge of the bluff across from the 800 block on North Broadway was torn down prior to 1872. The foundation only was visible at that date, which was the year I came to this city.

The various locations of the United States Customs offices in Corpus Christi are difficult to ascertain. The recollection of Mr. Eli Merriman, Mr. W.S. Rankin, Capt. Andy Anderson, all of whom I consulted, and my own recollections, are conflicting and uncertain. In 1870, I believe the office was in a cottage where the Palace Theater is now, on North Chaparral, with Dr. Kearney in charge. This house was later occupied by Dr. DeRyee and Dr. Turpin, about 1880. The following names are connected with the Customs Service here: Givens, Ranahan, Kearney, Swisher, Paschall, and Haines.

Ropes Pass was a channel across Mustang Island, made under the direction of Col. Ropes. Although some have believed to the contrary, the channel was actually cut all the way across the island.

Mr. Ropes made up a party to go over and celebrate the opening of the pass, poetically referring to the waters of the Gulf kissing the waters of the bay. Although the dredge had cut clear across the island, there was no current of water in the channel. A load of shovels had been brought along, and the entire party went to work and shoveled the sand, piling it up on each side, until finally the water from each end began to trickle in; and when the channels of water met, the waters of the Gulf actually kissed the waters of the bay. I was one of the party who helped with the shoveling.

Edward Harvey Caldwell (1851-1940) (Plate 17) was born in Cleveland, Tenn., the oldest of nine sons and one daughter born to Rev. and Mrs. William Edward Caldwell. In 1872, Rev. Caldwell became pastor of the First Presbyterian Church in Corpus Christi. His son Edward Harvey moved to Corpus Christi in March 1872. He worked as a clerk for Doddridge, Lott & Davis and turned to sheep ranching in Duval County in 1875. He served as a postmaster at Borjas and county commissioner of Duval County. He married Ada Lasater in 1880 and returned to Corpus Christi in 1884 to enter the hardware business (Plate 18). Caldwell was one of the founding members of the Commercial Club, which later became the Chamber of Commerce. Interview dates by Marie Blucher, from Nov. 18, 1938 to Dec. 21, 1939. E. H. Caldwell died on March 14, 1940 when he was 89 years old.

CHAPTER 7

WILLIAM S. RANKIN
WHEN I WAS YOUNG

I was a small boy and don't remember many incidents about the bombardment of Corpus Christi in 1862, but I do recall what happened one Sunday morning.

My mother and all the girls and I went to Episcopal church services, which were being held in a long frame building used now as a store, at the corner of Chaparral and Schatzell streets. Nathan Cohn had a business there later. Capt. Hobby[1] and maybe some of his soldiers were attending church that morning. Capt. Hobby was short and chunky, a fine-looking young fellow. A man, or perhaps even several men, came running in to the building and ran to Capt. Hobby, and you should have seen him and his men run out of that church. Word had come that the Yankees were going to bombard the town.

For safety our family, like many others, went to the country. We went out to Gallagher's Ranch, about two or three miles out of town — or it may have been four or five miles. The Gallaghers[2] had a sheep ranch at the time. We could hear the cannon all night. The FitzSimmons went out there, too. They had a store in town. We stayed out there a few days. One day another boy and I came in to

---

[1] The Confederate officer sent to prepare a defense of Corpus Christi was Maj. Alfred Marmaduke Hobby, whose family had settled at St. Mary's in 1857.
[2] Richard Gallagher and family.

the FitzSimmons store and got groceries and went back. The Gallaghers had plenty of meat and cornbread, I remember.

During these war days food was scarce in town, and we had to parch corn to make the coffee. Our home was at the corner of Mesquite and Lawrence streets.

One of my regular Saturday chores — I suppose you might call it — was to go with my brother out in the country, beyond where the Country Club is now, to a place on the left side of the road to get butter. We would take our time and play along the way. I don't remember the lady's name now. We got three pounds of butter for $1, nice country butter. She would give us each a great big slice of home-made bread and a big glass of buttermilk before we started back. We were probably eight or ten years old. As a rule we had several cows of our own; some families always had from one to three cows; I know the Beldens did.

Some of our fun as boys came from teasing old Dickie Power. I recall him as a somewhat eccentric man. It was his daily custom to go from his home on the bluff (at the corner of Broadway and Lipan) downtown every evening about dusk, say about seven o'clock, passing our home on the way.

Some of the neighborhood boys planned a joke on Mr. Power. The FitzSimmons boys from across the street and I made an imitation snake. It resembled the king snakes occasionally seen and greatly feared. To the tail end we fastened a large and noisy rattlesnake rattle and to the other end a very long string. We hid the snake in our garden just inside the fence and laid the string under the fence and across the street, where we all awaited the coming old Mr. Power. Soon we saw him and just before he reached the spot where the snake was hidden, we jerked the string, the snake darted across the sidewalk with a terrible rattle, and Mr. Power jumped back and screamed, "Snake! Snake!"

When he discovered the boys across the street and knew we had played a prank on him, he was very angry and threatened to whip us.

It wasn't all fun in Corpus, though. Sometime in the early 1860s, it must have been, because the yellow fever epidemic hadn't yet struck the town, when we had a terrible freeze in April. Some men were out on the bay in a sailboat when a fierce norther came up and capsized the boat. The men clung to the boat for safety, but as the temperature dropped to freezing their chances for rescue became very slim. One man — old man Rains — drowned or froze to death and another man died from the cold. One man named Bryant was in the group, but I don't remember whether he was lost or not. The boys, Ben Gibbs and his brother Jim, were badly frozen but were rescued and their lives saved.

In 1867 Corpus Christi was hit by a terrible epidemic of yellow fever. Hardly a family escaped the sickness. At our old home several of the family became sick. My oldest sister Agnes was well on the way to recovery and thought she ought to try to help with all the work there was to be done, so she told my mother she was going to cook breakfast one morning. Mother forbade it, but Agnes got up and helped anyway. She immediately had a relapse and died in two days.

Father was very ill with the fever but was apparently recovering. They gave him sweat baths, a usual method of treatment of yellow fever. They did everything to induce a profuse sweat, such as piling on the blankets and giving the patient some kind of hot tea. This caused considerable discomfort. Father's clothing was soaked, and the sweat even passed through the mattress. He begged for a change, but mother felt it would endanger his recovery to change bedding and clothing in the midst of sweating. A neighbor, who dropped in from her home nearby, begged mother to give father some relief. At last mother yielded. A relapse soon set in, the black vomit came on, and father died the next day.

Some time after this, some friends and I had spent the morning playing down at the bay. Returning home, I became sick at the stomach and got a headache. I soon had the yellow fever. My younger brother also took the fever and we were in bed together. My brother had only a light attack and was soon up again, but I was confined to bed for a while longer. I was not allowed to drink, only a small piece of ice on the tip of my tongue. One night I awoke, and by the dim light of the night lamp burning on the mantel I saw a pitcher and glass beside the lamp. Slipping out of bed, I quietly tiptoed over to the mantel and drank two glasses of water. I told no one what I had done, but apparently it did me no harm. I was soon well. Later on, I told my mother and she scolded me severely for the risk I had taken.

There was a man named Marsh living where the Methodist manse is now[3] whose two children, a boy and a girl, were ill with the fever. The father did not believe in treatment of the fever by withholding the drinking of water. As he had to go on with his work as usual, in spite of his sick children, he wrapped them up in a wet sheet and placed a pitcher of ice water by the side of the bed, telling them they could drink all they wanted, but not to get out of bed under any circumstances. In this case, too, the drinking of water seemed to do no harm, for both of the children recovered.

Mother's experience in nursing her own family through the yellow fever made her much sought after by others in distress when the dread disease descended upon a household. She was called in by various families to help. The William Headens sent their baby girl, Bessie, down to Mrs. Rankin to care for because of the fever in the Headen home. After a few days Mr. Headen came down to take the baby back, saying Mrs. Headen couldn't stand it any longer without seeing her baby. Mother protested, for she felt the exposure to the fever would surely result in the baby's catching it also. The baby was taken back to the home, however, and in two days she contracted the fever. It was not fatal, though, and she was soon well again.

Coffins for the victims were hastily made. They were usually plain boxes of pine covered with plain black cloth. Andrew Baldeschwiler was one of the men who made a great many of the coffins. The lumber intended for the Presbyterian Church on the bluff was on the ground, and some of this was used for making coffins.

As I grew up I learned the painter's trade. It happened that one day in 1875 I was painting upstairs on the McCampbell building. There were Charles Vandervoort, Chris Yung, McKenzie and I all painting together when John McClane and others came riding by

[3] Corner of Chaparral and Mann.

and calling out, "Mexican raid! Mexican raid!" We locked up the house and ran out. There was quite a bit of excitement. I had never carried a gun up to that time, but that night I was assigned with others to guard the outskirts of the city and was part of the armed patrol.

The McCampbell building was at the corner of Mesquite and Peoples streets, opposite the City Hall eastward. The John McCampbell family lived upstairs and the judge had his office up there. Downstairs there was a store. It seemed that everyone who went into business in that building failed until I went in. I know of at least four or five who failed.

When I asked for a lease for a couple of years, Mr. McCampbell, the owner, said, "You think you'll stay two years?" I made a success of it, though, staying there four and a half years and making good money there (Plate 23).[4]

McKenzie and I had the first paint store in Corpus Christi. It was known by the name of Rankin and McKenzie.[5] We handled paints and paint supplies, window panes, window shades, linoleum, etc. How different Corpus Christi was in those days. Just think how our fine streets and automobiles make travel so easy. When I was a boy and young man, there was no way to get across to Portland except to drive right through the water. The route was staked out, but sometimes it was hard to see the stakes. First you would start out straight, then you would zig-zag to the left, then zig-zag to the right, then you would go straight ahead again. If you didn't turn at the right place, you would go into about 15 feet of mud.

---

[4] Rankin operated a retail grocery store on the first floor of the McCampbell building.

[5] James McKenzie, Rankin's partner in the paint store, was known as Little Mac. He was struck and killed by a streetcar in the 1890s.

William S. (Bill) Rankin (1856-1948) (Plate 22). His parents, Mr. and Mrs. James T. Rankin, immigrated to Corpus Christi from Glasgow, Scotland in 1853. James Rankin ran a livery stable when William was born, one of eight children born to the Rankins. William began work as a painter and later owned a paint store with James McKenzie, then entered the retail grocery business. He built the Corpus Christi Bank Building in 1891 and was a major stockholder in the Miramar Hotel on North Beach, which burned soon after it opened. He married Louise Weideman of New Orleans in 1885. Rankin served as an elder in the First Presbyterian Church for 47 years. Date of interview by Marie Blucher: Feb. 24, 1939 to April 9, 1940. William S. Rankin died in 1948 when he was 92.

CHAPTER 8

ANNIE MARIE KELLY
REMINISCENCES

nnie Marie Kelly was born in England on May 4, 1857, of Irish parents, John Kelly and his wife. About 1863 or 1864, the family left England for the United States. They made their home, for a time at least, in Pittsburgh. Annie Marie remembered seeing the funeral train procession of Abraham Lincoln. She was hoisted up by her father to view it.[1]

In Pittsburgh were John Kelly's brother Dennis and his wife from Corpus Christi. Because of their Union sympathies, they left Corpus Christi at the outbreak of the Civil War. At the end of hostilities, they returned to their Texas home and John Kelly and family followed them, from Illinois, in 1867.

Annie Marie, her parents and sisters made the portion of the trip from Indianola to Corpus Christi on the mail boat which, she recalled, was no larger than a small sailing vessel. Although it had a cabin and provided sleeping accommodations for passengers, it seemed so small after the steamer on which they had reached Indianola, that Mrs. Kelly fearfully said, "Oh, John, we are all going to drown!" The captain of this boat was Mike Brennan.[2]

---

[1] Lincoln's funeral train, which left Washington on April 21, 1865, retraced the route he traveled as president-elect, except for the deletion of Pittsburgh and Cincinnati and the addition of Chicago on the 1,654-mile route. So the Kelly family must have seen the funeral train somewhere else in Pennsylvania, perhaps Harrisburg or Philadelphia, but not Pittsburgh.

[2] The mail boat was the *Agnes*.

The hazards of the journey safely over, the family settled down to make their home in a new land, but greater hazards were ahead. When the dread yellow fever struck Corpus Christi in 1867, it claimed as victims both John Kelly and his wife, leaving as orphans their five daughters, of whom the eldest was 12. These children made their home with their uncle, Martin Kelly, a brother of John. Martin and his wife Mary reared them tenderly.

Annie Marie said Corpus Christi was not much of a place when they came in 1867, the houses being very scattered. She remembered little of the public schools; she attended the convent school. The Catholic church was a small building facing west, located near where the St. Patrick's Cathedral was later built. She recalled the lighthouse on the bluff. "It was all open on one side, with a little ditch around it. We used to go inside the old lighthouse on our way to school and look around."

She recalled a Mexican raid.[3] "We were hidden in the brush. We were out at my Uncle Martin's ranch, about six miles in the country, at that time.[4] John Gallagher came riding out like a madman, saying the Mexicans were coming and were going to kill all of us. My uncle scattered us through the brush. I was never so scared in my life. My uncle would come to each of us in the brush every once in a while during the night to see how we were getting along. I thought daylight would never come. My Aunt Mary told me that some cowboys came along and stopped at the house. She made them coffee and kept giving them coffee to keep them there for protection. But finally they had to go. Those were terrible times. Shortly after the Mexican raid Murdock was murdered at his little store near the Oso. The murderers tied him to a plow in the store and set the house on fire."[5]

Annie Marie remembered another incident that impressed her deeply. "One morning early, as I was walking along, I looked up

---

[3] This must have been another raid, or fears of a raid, rather than the famous Nuecestown Raid in 1875 since it occurred before her marriage in 1873.

[4] Martin Kelly's ranch, called El Paiste Ranch or the Kelly Ranch, was southwest from where Cliff Maus Field was located later.

[5] William Murdock, who lived on the Santa Gertrudis Road outside Corpus Christi, was burned alive on Aug. 19, 1872.

and saw a man hanging out the window of the courthouse by a rope from the ceiling. I ran to the house of my uncle Dennis, the sheriff at the time, and called him. But the man was already dead. The murderers had broken into the jail after getting the keys from the sheriff, at the point of a gun, and had taken the prisoner and hanged him."

Not long after this Dennis Kelly was murdered. A man who had stolen a horse was standing near Kelly and Kelly, not knowing about the theft, said something to him in a joking way about stealing horses. The man put his arm around Kelly, drew his knife, and stabbed him. The man was never prosecuted. "Murder," Annie Marie said, was frequent in those days and many murderers were never brought to justice."[6]

About 1873 Annie Marie married Charles Alexander Lewis, a Confederate veteran and a descendant of the Meriwether Lewis family.

Mrs. Lewis recalled very well the two courthouses (Plate 21),[7] since she lived across the street from the courthouse square ever since she came to Corpus Christi. When asked if she ever had any unusual experiences crossing the reef north of town, she said that crossing the reef was not as bad as one might think. Some places were very shallow and others deep, but in no place along the marked route was it necessary for the horses to swim.[8]

Mrs. Lewis' home was one of the old houses in Corpus Christi, built by Martin Kelly in about 1857. The walls were of shell concrete, very thick, with high ceilings that showed the wooden beams. The doors were made of wide boards running up and down. The dining room was added later, filling what was formerly an open court to which each of the rooms of the house had access by doors and steps. There were no bathrooms or closets in the original house;

---

[6] Sheriff Dennis Kelly was stabbed to death on June 13, 1870.

[7] The original 1853 Nueces County Courthouse and the so-called Hollub Courthouse that replaced it in 1875 (Plate 20).

[8] Other accounts say that at high tide horses had to swim across a small section of the reef by Rincon Point on North Beach. A cut in the reef was made by Army engineers when Zachary Taylor's army was encamped at Corpus Christi in 1845.

they were added later. There was a concrete water cistern in the yard. During the Civil War, the house was occupied by Martin Kelly and family. When Corpus Christi was bombarded by Union ships, three cannonballs passed through the roof of the house and through the kitchen wall.[9]

During the storm of 1919, the family went up on the hill for safety. The house suffered only slight damage. Two window panes were broken and the doors were swollen. Most of the old furniture was washed away and never recovered, except for a lovely marble-topped walnut table, five chairs and a few other pieces. The old concrete cistern in the yard weathered the storm, but it was demolished about 1926 after a small boy nearly drowned in it.

Annie Marie Lewis was given a life interest in the old house, according to the will of her cousin Hannah, a daughter of Dennis Kelly. Hannah provided for Mrs. Lewis in this manner and stipulated that at her death the property was to pass into the hands of the Catholic Church.

Mrs. Charles Alexander Lewis, nee Annie Marie Kelly, (1857-1940) left Liverpool, England with her parents and sisters when she was six or seven years old. Both parents died in the yellow fever epidemic in Corpus Christi in 1867. She and her four sisters were reared by her uncle, Martin Kelly and his wife Mary. Mrs. Lewis and her husband had six children: two daughters, Josephine, Lenora, and four sons, J. J. Lewis, F. L. Lewis, W. E. Lewis and A. C. Lewis. She was interviewed at her home on Mesquite Street, across from the Courthouse, on March 2, 1939. She died on Feb. 9, 1940 and was buried in San Diego, Texas, where she had resided with her husband until his death in 1914.

---

[9] Annie Marie's daughter, Mrs. L. L. Sherman, once recalled that the old cannonballs remained about the house for years.

CHAPTER 9

THOMAS NOAKES
THE BANDIT RAID OF 1875

From the numerous murders and raids that had been made within the last two years, I deemed it necessary to be well prepared for such an emergency when my time came, which I always had a presentiment it would do. I used all my time in making preparations for the event and went to great expense in planning the trench under the store.

I shaped the trench so that a person being in it was perfectly safe from shots fired from the outside. I could reach it from three trap doors, one in the floor at my bed, one at my desk in the store, and it led to a way of escape at the back of the house, which saved my life. A branch also led to the cellar and another from the cellar to the front of the new stoop.

At the trap door in the side room I could reach the top of the house by means of a hidden ladder. In the top of the house I kept a needle gun with 500 cartridges. I had, to the best of my recollection, 16 improved pistols and 50 boxes of cartridges distributed around the house, and with sufficient warning of their approach to enable me to close the house, I considered myself capable of fighting off 12 or 15 men. I had determined never to surrender to a force no smaller.

On Good Friday, March 26, 1875, I was kept busy all day, having remittances to make to several business houses, that I wanted to send by the evening mail for goods that I had received a few days before, and if they had been sent off sooner I should have owed no man a cent.

The day before the raid,[1] my boys and I worked very hard completing fences, making a small field to cultivate, and a pasture which I intended to plant with Bermuda grass. This, together with the bridge over the gully west of my place, and the wharf and warehouse on the river, finished the plans I had made ten years before, with the additional satisfaction of knowing that everything was paid for. We had pinched ourselves up to this time in our domestic affairs to enable us to carry out our plans.

I now concluded that for the future we could afford to live and eat generally in a more liberal manner than had been our wont and we hoped to get some little enjoyment out of life. Such enjoyment, however, was never to be ours. By sundown the same evening, everything in and about the house, store and warehouse,[2] everything we valued in this world except our lives, was wiped out, gone, and as the day had been warm we were but half-clad and the children without shoes, and no home to shelter us or food to eat.

After finishing my letters, I made up the mail in readiness for the carrier who was about due, when a man named John Smith[3] came to the store for some flour and while in the act of handing him a parcel over the counter, I saw three Mexicans ride up and fasten their horses to the rack in front of the store and excitedly approach the door, heavily armed. I said nothing to Smith of the circumstances, but walked hastily to the sitting room at the back of the store to get my Winchester rifle, thinking that things looked shaky.

I no sooner got my rifle in hand when Smith came rushing into the room closely followed by a savage looking Mexican who had his gun in an attitude to shoot Smith, but immediately on seeing me

---

[1] It was variously called the Nuecestown Raid or the Noakes Raid.

[2] The Noakes store at Nuecestown, also known as The Motts, was on a hill 200 yards from the river.

[3] He was called Windy Smith and sometimes called Lying Smith.

brought it around on me. But before he could shoot my bullet had perforated his chest and knocked all the fight out of him.

In the meantime, Smith escaped out of a door opposite the one by which he had entered the room, and my wife passing in as he went out, was with me in the room. Seeing the wounded Mexican could shoot no more, I made ready for the next to follow him. Having seen but three Mexicans I felt no apprehension as to my being able to cope with that number and expected that when they heard the firing they would come to the assistance of their comrade. But none coming, I stepped to the door leading into the store to see where they were and taking aim at the fellow nearest me when my attention was attracted by a great number of Mexicans outside the front of the store. There appeared to me to be at least a hundred.

Realizing that I was overpowered (for one man cannot, with much hope of success, fight a hundred), I did not fire, but turned, expecting to see my wife in the room, but she was nowhere to be found, and the doors and windows looking from three sides of the room where I was, all being open, and the Mexicans taking up positions to surround us, I was compelled to avail myself of a trap-door through the floor, by which I passed into the trench. This trench enabled me to pass from one part of the house to another and get into any room I wanted to without being exposed to sight.

I found Smith, who, crawling under the house at the back, had found the trench. He was very excited and I advised him to stay where he was and keep quiet and that I would go to the front of the house and see if there was any chance to fight them off when, if I saw he could do any good with it, I would furnish him with a pistol. Excited as he was, he was best without one.

On reaching the trench from which I could see the crowd out in front of the store, I noticed several Americans held as prisoners. Among them was a man named Lane, a Dunn and another one named Nelson.[4] I came to the conclusion that the Mexicans meant

---

[4] Jim Lane, Mike Dunn, and Tom Nelson were captured by the bandits at a cow camp on the Nueces. Other captives taken on the roads were S. G. Borden, H. A. Gilpin, Fred Franks, Joe Howell, Mrs. E. D. Sidbury and her daughter, Mrs. R. R. Savage, Miss Laura Allen, George Reynolds, his two teenage daughters and their governess, Miss Adele DeBerry.

to take all the prisoners they could from among the Americans and as soon as they were through robbing have the enjoyment of a general massacre, a la Peñescal.[5] I determined that I would not be taken alive, so passed back to a place where I could command the store with my rifle, but to my consternation I found my wife in the store, surrounded by the raiders, and two of them placed in such a way, with cocked pistols, that any shot that should be fired from any unseen party would be retaliated on her by one of the fiends. Consequently, to resume firing was only to insure her being shot and I had to remain inactive while my wife was trying to persuade them not to carry out the threat of taking me to the burning house. Several times after they lit a fire in the store, my wife put it out, the first time by throwing a pitcher of water on it.[6]

I noticed that Smith had left the trench and hearing shots from the direction in which he must have gone, knew that he was shot down by the guards placed to keep us from leaving the house. I could hear the roar of fire over my head and to remain longer was certain death. My only chance lay in shooting down the Mexican who guarded the back of the house and make my escape in the smoke. When I reached the end of the trench from which to put my design in operation, my wife called to me that the Mexicans were not there and now was my chance to leave alive. She helped pull me through a hole in the fence. When I left her she was getting a featherbed out of the house and in spite of the impending danger I could not but feel amused at such a notion as getting out a bed while thousands of other articles, in my estimation, would have had the preference.

I expected every minute to be fired upon and in such a case had made up my mind to lie flat and return the fire, but I was allowed to turn the corner of the fence without molestation. By keeping along the other angle of the fence I reached a point where to go farther I

---

[5] The year before, on May 9, 1874, at Peñascal, a small settlement at Baffin Bay, store owner John Morton, his brother and two customers were killed in a cold-blooded massacre by bandits.

[6] Several accounts of the raid reported that one bandit quirted, or lashed with a whip, Marie Noakes, but her husband does not mention this in his version of the raid.

had to pass open ground where I would be seen. I concluded to remain and see it out. I passed by Smith soon after leaving the house. He was sprawled face-down and covered with blood and I thought he was dead. The Mexicans not seeing me leave boasted they had burned me with the house, as was their intention.

When I watched from my trench the crowd in front of the store, I noticed that the mail rider was among the prisoners. They took him as he came up to deliver his mail and he was not allowed to perform his duty, but he and both his horses were carried off by them, together with the mail bags.

My wife tells me that when she left the house, as she ran down the hill towards the river, the two Mexicans who had shot Smith rode after her and were preparing to shoot her, but she begged them to spare her for the sake of her baby, and they let her go. Early in the attack my wife had given the baby to my little daughter and her brother, both together being hardly able to carry the youngest, telling them to carry him away as quickly as they could, and the three had about reached the point where the Mexicans shot Smith and were witnesses of the deed and from what they saw became so horrified that they fell to the ground, incapable of moving. In the meantime the two older boys, who had been on the river and knew nothing of what was going on, suspected something was wrong at the house, having seen the Mexicans shoot down Smith. They caught sight of the little ones and seeing them fall came to their rescue. All agreed that while crossing the flats the five were fired at by the Mexicans, and one of the shots intended for Smith nearly hit Grace, the little girl. The children reached the river and crossed in a skiff, where my wife joined them sometime later.

As soon as darkness set in the Mexicans turned loose all of their prisoners except the mail-rider and two or three others, among whom was W. A. Ball, our justice of the peace, whom I afterwards learned they took with them some distance before they allowed him to escape. As soon as the Mexicans were gone I went to Smith, whom I found alive, but with so many bullet holes in him that death seemed inevitable. I now met my wife who told me that the children were all safe, which made me feel very grateful. Smith was about 200 yards from the house and crying for water. I went to the place where the house had stood with the idea of getting water, but of course everything was gone or red-hot. I could find nothing that would hold water. While I was hunting for something in which to carry water, two men, strangers, rode up to the fire on the other side and one of them requested me to approach the fence. As soon as I was close to him he demanded my rifle, at the same time covering me with his six-shooter and threatening to kill me unless I complied with his demands.[7]

Not dreaming of such conduct from a white man, I was totally unprepared and he could have shot me before I refused his request, saying that I needed the rifle for my own and my family's protection. However, as he insisted that he could do more good with it than I could, as he was going in pursuit of the Mexicans, I gave the rifle to him on his promise that he would return it, but, poor fellow, in less than an hour he was dead, and only through luck I recovered the rifle, which was picked up near his body by F. Sims. The person who took the rifle was named Swank, I was told, and was at the front during the pursuit of the Mexicans and was reported at the time to have been killed by them. He was a brave man and it was a pity there was not more like him.

I now returned to Smith. He would not let me leave him although I had no hat or clothes to keep me warm. After a while Nesties brought a cart and took him away. Then we hunted up the little ones, who were by this time huddled together under a fence near the ruins, crying and half-witted from fright. Marie had luckily pulled the running gear of the light wagon out of reach of the flames and we now took the hind wheels and mustered up all our possessions, which consisted of a bed, a blanket, and a quilt, which Marie had carried out while the house was burning. With these and the sewing machine and the five little ones, we started down the hill to the warehouse I had recently built on the river, and in the darkness took possession of the only home we now owned. Three days before, the warehouse had been full of flour, meal, coffee, sugar, and groceries. I had worked hard to get it all up to the store

---

[7] This member of the posse was a roofer or carpenter from Corpus Christi named George Swank.

just in time to get it burned. Now we had not so much as a bite of bread.

While the house was burning I had to stand and watch from my retreat by the fence the huge tongues of flames shoot heavenward, knowing they were licking up the fruits of ten years toil and everything, except ourselves, that I valued in the world. I never experienced so maddening a feeling as that which came over me when I realized that my children were crying for the want of a roof to cover them because of those bloodthirsty fiends.

Thomas John Noakes (1829-1878) (Plate 24) was born at Sussex, England. He came to Texas in 1845 and worked for a time for Henry Kinney, the founder of Corpus Christi. Noakes was well-educated and developed skills as a carpenter, saddle-maker, gunsmith, musical instrument repairman, farmer, and storekeeper. He taught school for a time. He married Maria (he called her Marie) von Ludwig and they had seven children: Thomas John Jr., Nelson Edmondson, Grace, Adolph, Leona, Mary, who died in infancy, and New, who was the baby at the time of the raid. Noakes kept a diary. The first volume was lost but the second volume, which begins in 1858, and later volumes tell us much about life in Texas during the Civil War. A hand-transcribed copy of Noakes' diary is in the Corpus Christi Central Library. Noakes' account of the 1875 raid was printed in the Corpus Christi Caller on Dec. 22, 1912 and later reprinted in Frontier Times and the Texas Historical Association Quarterly. After the raid, Noakes built a new store a mile west of the old location and the town moved with him. In time, Nuecestown was supplanted by Calallen. Thomas John Noakes died in 1878 and was buried on his farm outside Nuecestown.

CHAPTER 10

MRS. DELMAS GIVENS RECOLLECTIONS

Mary Elizabeth Manly at the age of 19 left her native state of North Carolina to visit her cousin, Mrs. Ed Buckley, in Corpus Christi. She arrived here Nov. 21, 1876, on the steamer *Mary*, this trip being the last made by the *Mary* to this city, as on the next voyage the ill-fated steamer foundered on Aransas bar.[1]

Mary Manly had good opportunity to become well-acquainted with her fellow passengers aboard the ship. The steamer was forced to remain on the Aransas bar for about three days due to low water over the bar. It was just like a house party, she said, with everybody having a good time. One of the passengers in particular attracted her attention, as he sketched nearly every person on the boat. He was a caricaturist named McKay, or some name similar to that, from Cuero. Other passengers were Mrs. Fullerton, the mother of Mrs. Perry Doddridge, Mr. and Mrs. Sullivan, who later moved to San Antonio, and a Mr. Debreau of Montreal, Canada.

The Ed Buckleys, whom the young traveler was to visit, lived where the Princess Louise Hotel is now, at the corner of Water and Twigg streets. One week after Miss Manly reached Corpus Christi,

---

[1] The Morgan Line side-wheel steamer *Mary* sank on Nov. 30, 1876. For years, parts of the sunken ship showed above the water near the Aransas Pass channel before the remains of the wreck were dynamited.

a Firemen's Ball was given at Market Hall (Plate 25), and Mrs. Buckley insisted that she attend it, as it was the biggest affair of the year here. Although a stranger in the town, she had a good time at the ball, where she met several of her fellow passengers from the *Mary*, among them the caricaturist. He had his portfolio of drawings with him and showed them to her that evening, to her great enjoyment but to the chagrin of one who looked over their shoulders and saw himself portrayed in a comical aspect.

At the ball, Miss Manly danced many times with Major Downing. "We were a queer couple. He was as big as a house and I was no bigger than a sparrow. But it was Mr. Sidney Gail Borden who took me in to supper."

Miss Manly's first few weeks centered around the Buckley home and that of Mr. and Mrs. J. B. Murphy, who lived at the north end of the same block on Water Street. Other friends were soon made, however, and she no longer felt a stranger in the town.

Ed Buckley bought wool for a New York firm and on one of his periodic trips into the country he took his wife, four children, their nurse, and their guest, Miss Manly. They traveled in two hacks, which were called carriages in North Carolina. With them was an escort of Texas Rangers. James Bryden was also with them and surveyor John Caldwell.[2]

All were welcome guests at whatever ranch they approached. Some places they stayed overnight and at others several days. On this trip, which was in 1877, Mrs. Givens recalled the delightful time spent at the Sullivan home in San Patricio, at George Reynolds' ranch, at Frank Shaeffer's, and in Echo, where they stayed at Pat Murphy's.

The visit to Texas, which had been planned to last a year, was extended from time to time and four years after her arrival in Corpus Christi, she married Delmas Givens, a young lawyer. The wedding ceremony was performed by Father St. John,[3] one of the

---

[2] He was better known as Lafayette Caldwell. His map of 1879 shows large ranches, or pastures, and public roads of Nueces County.

[3] She was probably referring to Father St. Jean.

beloved priests of the Catholic Church. Mrs. Givens made her home here for the remainder of her life.

Corpus Christi's appearance in 1876 made such a vivid impression upon Mary Manly, when she arrived, that she never forgot it. At that time Corpus Christi was very small indeed; an outstanding impression made upon the young visitor was that of the raggedy-taggedy appearance of the horses and the hacks. A few families, she said, had fine horses, among them Mrs. John Rabb, and the Doddridges, but the general appearance of horses here was very poor.

The nicest looking and best-kept place in the city in 1876 was the home of Mr. and Mrs. A. M. Davis at the corner of North Broadway and Antelope streets. Mrs. Davis was a sister of Uriah Lott. The house next to this on the north was a little concrete house, with a concrete cistern near it and was occupied by Mrs. Sinclair. Mrs. Sinclair was a sister of George Evans. Born Mary Moore, she had been married to Mr. Jones before she became Mrs. Sinclair. The third house from the corner of Antelope and Broadway was the home of former Governor E. J. Davis, which had been sold to Col. Norwick Gussett who lived there with his family. The house had been brought in from Britton Motts[4] near the Oso. It consisted of only three or four rooms and had a long front gallery and a long dining room. Some time after 1880, Mr. Gussett had it remodeled so his daughters would have a nice home. A second story was added and other changes made, but the front rooms downstairs were not altered. Miss Leona Gussett married Royal Givens in the new part of the home.

At the corner of North Broadway and Leopard streets, where the Plaza Hotel is now, Uriah Lott had a house.[5] Capt. Kenedy bought it from Mr. Lott and gave it to his daughter, Mrs. Arthur Spohn. The captain had wanted to buy the corner where the Nixon Building

---

[4] Anna Moore Schwien, a former slave of the Britton family, said the E. J. Davis home was built of new lumber, not from lumber moved from the Britton Ranch.

[5] This was also known as the Redmond cottage, built by John Redmond and later occupied by his son, Dr. Henry Redmond. It was torn down to make way for the White Plaza Hotel.

is now, but the owner would not sell. He then bought the Dowd place farther south, at the corner of Lipan and North Broadway, where the Cathedral Hall is now, Capt. Kenedy's own home having stood there before the Hall.

Mrs. John Rabb, owner of a fine ranch, had a beautiful home on Broadway near Lipan; she named the place Magnolia Mansion (Plate 11). This home, after changing owners many times, is now the Catholic Cathedral Hall and stands at the corner in the first block south of its original location.

Mrs. Givens' husband had an uncle here, John S. Givens, a prominent lawyer, at one time a partner of John S. McCampbell. The John Givens family lived at the corner of North Broadway and Blucher (formerly Chatham) streets, where the telephone building is now. In 1876 this home had three rooms, not including the dining room and kitchen, for these were out in the yard at some distance from the house. These two rooms were old and built of concrete, and it was said at that time that some of General Taylor's men had lived there. John Givens had built the three-room house in which the family lived. Later he added a second story to his home, which was eventually bought by Mr. Atlee McCampbell.

Recalling early days and friends, Mrs. Givens said that in 1880 there was quite a storm here. The Murphy place on the shoreline was nearly washed away, the water coming up over the yard. Soon after the high water, when Judge Murphy was out of town, Mrs. Murphy, having decided she wanted to move to the bluff, made arrangements to buy the property on Antelope Street, between North Broadway and Carancahua streets, four lots, belonging to A. M. Davis. A purchase price of $3,000 was agreed upon. When Mr. Murphy returned he was so opposed to moving from their home on the beach that the plan was given up. After his death, however, Mrs. Murphy bought the same property for herself, but she had to pay $6,000 for it. She wanted to start a marine hospital there; but as she received no encouragement she gave up her plans and moved to San Antonio. (The four lots referred to are now the site of the post office.)

J. B. Murphy was mayor of Corpus Christi about 1882 and 1883. The outstanding accomplishment of his first year was the purchase of the Market Hall building from Mr. Hoffman, the city paying $1,500 for it. By this purchase the city was relieved of the expense of monthly rent. The property upon which the building stood had been given to the city for a market place; and as the city had no market place when they bought the building, the original intention for a market was carried out through the purchase, as the city put stalls which were rented for the same of such miscellaneous things as poultry and meat, besides other market items (Plate 25).[6] The city made money on it. Mr. Murphy ran for mayor a second time and was elected, but he never got over the excitement of the race and died soon after the election.

Mary Elizabeth (Manly) Givens (1857-1940) was born in North Carolina of an educated and prominent family. Her grandfather Manly was the governor of North Carolina and the founder of Chapel Hill University. Mary Elizabeth came to Corpus Christi in November 1876, when she was 18 years old, for a 12-month visit. She stayed with a cousin, Mrs. Ed Buckley, the wife of a prominent wool merchant in Corpus Christi. Four years later, in 1880, she married a Corpus Christi lawyer, Delmas Givens Sr., who was the city attorney at the time. They had a son, William Delmas Givens Jr., in 1883. Date of Interview by Marie Blucher — Sept. 21, 1939 when Mrs. Givens was 82 years old. Dee Woods' interview of Mrs. Givens was published in the *Corpus Christi Caller* on Dec. 10, 1939. Her husband Delmas died in 1937 and Mrs. Givens died on Jan. 18, 1940.

---

[6] Stalls for butchers and fruit and vegetable vendors on the ground floor were always part of the original feature of Market Hall from its beginning, when Jordan and Rogers built it in 1871.

CHAPTER 11

RUTH DODSON
JUDGE GILPIN
THE PENITAS RANCH

Since this must be entirely from memory and most of it hear-say, it must be considered from that viewpoint. When Dr. Ashley had charge of the Writers Project at Corpus Christi, he wrote to me in regard to some of the early-day history. I tried to get him interested in doing research along the lines of the activities of Judge Gilpin, but he didn't seem interested. But he did tell me that Judge Gilpin was born in New York, but my father, who was alive at that time, said that the judge told him he was born in Halifax, Nova Scotia. My father,[1] whose memory never failed him and who was always very accurate, will be my authority for most of this.

Henry Alfred[2] (I think) Gilpin (Plate 29) — the Mexicans called him Don Enriquez — signed his name as H. A. Gilpin. He was born in Halifax, Nova Scotia, in May, 1808.[3] He was working in a bank in the United States — New Jersey, I think — when he left, suddenly my father thought. He came to Corpus Christi on a tramp steamer[4] in 1829, claiming later to be the first white man to land on

---

[1] Milton Dodson, owner of Rancho Perdido.

[2] His middle name was Addington.

[3] He was born on May 13, 1808, in Newport, R. I. His father, John Bernard Gilpin, from Halifax, Nova Scotia, was a British consul in Rhode Island.

[4] A schooner from New Orleans, loaded with trade goods for Mexico.

the coast. A Mr. Whalen[5] claimed to have been there earlier. However, Gilpin didn't remain any longer than the steamer did. I don't know where he went from there, but I do know that he must have spent some time in the vicinity of Houston at some time. I heard my father say that the judge told him that at the time they plowed with young buffaloes in the Houston part of the country. My father treated it as something of a joke, but since I have found through reading that it was a fact — that they did catch young buffalo and hitch them to plows.

Judge Gilpin spent a good deal of time in Mexico and spoke Spanish fluently, and could read and write it.[6] I think he had come to Corpus Christi in about 1848, or about the time the town incorporated.[7] I don't think he had any connection with Taylor's army. I asked my father one time what the judge was doing in Mexico before he came to Corpus Christi and he, very laconically said, "smuggling." I was somewhat shocked, but when I asked for an explanation, I found it wasn't such a bad sort of smuggling, somewhat like our old-time mavericking.

It appears that Gilpin held every public office of importance in Nueces County at one time or another. He was among the first, if not the first, chief justice (county judge) of Nueces County,[8] from which came his title of "Judge." For several years he represented his district in the State Congress.[9] I had a book that he gave me that had his name and address at Austin in it. The date was 1881.

Early in his time in Corpus Christi, he and two other men formed the mercantile partnership of Gilpin, Belden and Mann.[10] As

---

[5] Whelan, a shipwrecked sailor, landed in 1824 on the shore of where Corpus Christi would later be located, five years before Gilpin landed there.

[6] He worked with an American trader in Matamoros, Frederick Belden, who later relocated to Corpus Christi.

[7] That was in 1852.

[8] Gilpin was not the first. When Nueces County was organized on Jan. 11, 1847, Jose de Alba was the chief justice, with commissioners William Mann, George Brundrett, and Richard Powers. Gilpin's business partner, Frederick Belden, was the second chief justice, starting in 1848, which gained him the title in the Hispanic community of "El Juez."

[9] Legislature.

[10] Frederick Belden and William Mann.

was usual in the history of early-day merchants, they had ranching interests, too. This ranching interest was carried on in connection with their merchandising. I don't know when the merchandising partnership was discontinued.

My grandfather came to the west side of the Nueces River and settled at what now is Dinero in 1858, when my father was 19 years old. During that year, my father said he was on the location of what was the headquarters of the Belden Ranch, called Carmel,[11] which is now the Dean Miller Ranch. From there, he said, he went with Ben Dix, the foreman, the *caporal,* to Penitas.

I asked him if the judge had built his home there as early as then and he said he had. And the Mann Ranch was on the location of what became the Wade Ranch. Now, I don't know if they had formally divided their ranch interest then or not. But I do know that each maintained their residence in Corpus Christi, too. I asked my father what Penitas was like then and he said there were just a few Mexican houses there; I suppose just vaqueros for the Gilpin and Belden interest. I don't think Mann remained in business with them until Belden died,[12] which broke up the partnership of Gilpin and Belden.

Of course the Civil War coming on put a stop to much of the ranching over the country. I don't know whether the 800 acres of land that Judge Gilpin had was all that was ever in the tract or not, but you know that the Benton land, as we knew it, was state or county land until 1881 when Benton acquired it. And since this land came up close to Gilpin's home, the greater part of Penitas, as I remember it, must have been on this land that didn't belong to Gilpin at any time. I am not so sure that a small part might not have belonged to another person other than the public at some time. I am sure the graveyard is not on what was Judge Gilpin's land.

Now I will bring my people in. After my father came home from the war, he, of course, like all the rest had to go to work on horseback. In 1866 a young man who had made his headquarters at

---

[11] Named for Frederick Belden's hometown of Carmel, N.Y. After it was sold to Cornelius Cox, he called it El Colimal.

[12] Belden died on March 18, 1867.

Oakville, Martin Culver (Plate 27) — a half-brother to my mother — bought a bunch of cattle and hired Papa to help gather them. That was the beginning of the spectacular rise of Martin Culver. They moved the cattle in early 1867 to the location of our old home, only a short distance from Penitas. There was a small lumber house there, built by some men from Corpus, but given up during the war.

The range was free; even such land that had been acquired by someone, such as Gilpin and Belden, was unfenced. Uncle Martin became a very wealthy man in, I counted it up, seven years. My father was his foreman. In 1868, my mother,[13] when she was 20 years old, came from San Antonio to visit her brother and his family, and in 1869 she married the foreman. Uncle Martin had bought the land the house was on from Gilpin and Belden. He gave my father a few acres on the other side of the creek, and Papa bought a lumber house and put it there. It is known as the Chapa place. My oldest sister, Mrs. Joe Reynolds, was born at the main house, but my two brothers, Martin and Archie, were born at the Chapa place. In August, 1876, Papa bought Rancho Perdido from Uncle Martin and a month after they moved in, I was born there.

Uncle Martin went broke and finally died in Kansas. Now all of this is by way of saying that Judge Gilpin was our neighbor from the early days. He was there when my people came to that part of the country, but he spent a good deal of time in Corpus Christi. He was a polished man, and one of the most cultured and best educated of anyone who was ever in our part of the country.

The first store in Penitas was out to the west of the Judge's house. I have heard it called the Henderson Williams store — the family lived over the store, I think. I have never been on the spot, but, they say, the old underground cistern is there. When that store was discontinued, another one was built toward our place, probably a mile from the old Chapa place. I remember that store, but after the last merchant was about ready to close out and go back to Corpus Christi. At one time the mail was kept there, but I am inclined to think it was something of a rural route. The mail was brought from

---

[13] Susanna Burris.

Corpus Christi, taken along over the hills around by Penitas and to Lagarto. I don't remember the time, but Mrs. McNeill said they used to get their mail there. I think the Wades came to the ranch in about 1879, so it was about that time. There was never any school there. There was a little church, but was not used after I could remember. The priest used to come by our house and have church.

Outside of Judge Gilpin's house and the one his cook lived in, which was near his house, there were two little two-room houses off toward the east that belonged to the Judge, then the abandoned church, which they called the *capia,* the chapel, and where different transients lived at different times; then there was what had been a rather attractive — for those times — two-room house in what might have been the center of the town, if there had been a town, that had been built by an American, a gambler, before my time. Other than these, there were only *jacals,* and not many of them. There was a time, my father said, when Uncle Martin employed as many as 100 vaqueros, drawn mostly from the Penitas population, but that population scattered up and down the creek for a good distance. Living at the foot of those hills in front of our old home, before my time, was a man who was a silversmith. One would scarcely imagine one so employed living there now.

In an article that I have written for a book of reminiscences that I hope to finish some time, I tell of the smallpox outbreak that affected Penitas so sorely. It means that there was scarcely a family that escaped. It was in 1872 — Martin Dodson was a baby. A show came to Penitas. Shortly after it left, Mama said, a baby that belonged to a family that lived nearby seemed to be sick. She saw the baby and handled it, to see if she could do anything for it. The next morning she sent Trinidad — a young Mexican man who was working for her, and whom I have written up since I knew him in his old age in Alice — to see how the baby was. Trinidad came back very much excited — he had had smallpox in Mexico and knew what it was — and reported that the baby was broken out with smallpox. That was the beginning. They thought Martin might take it, so Trinidad fixed up a room where he expected to isolate himself with the baby, in case he did, but he escaped. Mama said there was funeral after funeral and the graveyard that had only a few graves became almost full. They wouldn't bury outside the graveyard because the ground hadn't been blessed, so it was not unusual to dig someone up when they were burying a new one. You know Mexicans think if one is afraid of catching something, they will catch it, so most of them were afraid to be afraid, so it resulted in those who were left behind being well pockmarked. When they seemed to ignore the instructions that Papa gave that no one of them were to come about the house, he had to threaten to shoot the first one that came inside the yard gate. He did have Trinidad catch up every cow that could be milked, and take the milk to a certain tree where those who had sick people would hang up their little tin buckets and Trinidad would put milk in them. The storekeeper at the little store took the smallpox, but survived.

Outside of the usual run of Mexicans being buried in the graveyard at Penitas, there has been only one American buried there. My aunt, Uncle Martin's wife, was of the Pugh family who lived in the Gussettville[14] community. She had a brother, Bill Pugh, who was afflicted with tuberculosis. He had a wife and some small children, the oldest child, a girl, was 12 years old; the youngest, a boy two years old. They were very poor, although the father seemed to be a man of considerable property. However, Aunt Kate felt that she could care for her brother better than he could be cared for at his home, so had him brought to her home. I don't know how long he lingered here at Uncle Martin's home. Papa, Mama and the little girl were living at the Chapa house. When Bill Pugh was nearing death, the entire Pugh family must have been at Uncle Martin's — the death of Bill Pugh was a legend I grew up with. I will have to date the death of the man with the birth of Martin, since that is the way I remember it. He died only two or three days before Martin was born — in February 1872. The house, as it became by the time I remember it, was being built (Plate 28). Uncle Martin had a carpenter working on it two years. At this time, the door in what we

---

[14] Gussettville was first called Fox Nation, after the Fox family, but in the 1850s the name was changed in honor of Norwick Gussett, owner of a general store there and later a wealthy wool merchant in Corpus Christi.

always called "the middle room" was not hung, so Bill Pugh was laid out on this — that ought to be material for one haunting.

Now, under ordinary circumstances, Bill Pugh should have been taken back to Gussettville[15] to be buried, but conditions were so unfavorable at the time that it was decided to bury him at Penitas. Papa said that a terrible cold spell had come up, and, of course, Mama's condition made it impossible for Uncle Martin and Aunt Kate to leave. At any rate, they buried Bill Pugh at Penitas, expecting to take him to Gussettville later. I don't know at what time Uncle Martin decided to have the rock wall built around the grave, but it must have been when he felt that the remains would not be taken back.

Now, through the years, Mama often spoke of Bill Pugh being buried at Penitas, and felt that the least his people could do was visit his grave, but not one of them ever did. She always wanted him moved to where his people could visit. One day while my father was living here with me, 60 years after the death of Bill Pugh, here came his son, who was the baby when his father died, and his daughter, a Mrs. Thelma Lindholm, a schoolteacher at George West, and also his sister, who was the 12-year-old daughter when Bill Pugh died. The son, Charles Pugh, I think it was, wanted Papa to tell him how to reach the place where his father was buried. Of course he could never have found the place alone, so Papa directed him to the ranch, where he, fortunately, found Kilmer at home, and who took them to the Penitas graveyard.

There is a little story involved in the call of Mrs. Lindholm at our old home. She acquired an iron pot that had been in our family for at least 60 years, but which her great-grandmother had brought from Ireland.

Mrs. Lindholm wrote to me that they had taken pictures of the grave. I don't know how soon after that visit of the relatives to Bill Pugh's grave, nor whether the visit had anything to do with it, but it was a very short time after that, that Kilmer came over and told me

---

[15] A number of Pughs were buried in the Gussettville Cemetery, a few miles southwest of George West. St. Joseph's Catholic Church is located on the grounds of the cemetery.

to write to Charlie Pugh that Mexicans told him that his father's grave had been dug into and for him to come and see about it. As soon as my letter could have reached Charlie Pugh, he was seen going through Mathis on the way to the grave. He had his son with him, I was told. Kilmer never went about the grave, but I saw someone — possibly Mr. John Stech, who told me that he heard that the grave had been dug into and he went to see it before it was filled up again. From what he told me, those who dug directed their digging toward the body — I thought they might have thought there was buried money in the corner of the enclosure — but it seemed that the idea was to reach the body, of which there were only a few bones and a little lumber of the coffin. One day I heard my father talking to himself, muttering: "To think of anyone digging into the grave of poor Bill Pugh expecting to find money!

"I guess I attended as many as a half-dozen funerals at that graveyard.

Back to Judge Gilpin. Several years ago I wrote a little sketch of the old man, very incomplete, which was published in the *Southwest Review*, and I have also written an article for my collection of reminiscences. But the thing that has always been a dream to me was to see the Penitas Ranch restored to what it was as I remember it. I always thought that if I ever got rich I would do the restoring myself. To me it was the most attractive place I had ever seen. I think I shall tell you right here about Mr. Graham.

Mr. Graham[16] came to this part of the country from Louisiana with Mr. S. G. Miller. In the early 1870s Mr. Miller sent him to Uncle Martin with a letter of introduction and telling him that he would stand responsible for Mr. Graham to the extent of ten thousand dollars. Uncle Martin was driving cattle to Rockport at the time, and put Mr. Graham in charge of that work. I don't know how it came about, but Judge Gilpin offered Mr. Graham a home with him. Probably this was somewhat later and at the time when Mr. Graham began working at the store at Penitas. At any rate, Mr. Graham, from time to time, dealt in horses, even within my memory. But I can't remember when his home was not with Judge

---

[16] S.D. Graham.

186

Gilpin. They were well suited to be company to each other, although Mr. Graham was very much younger. So Mr. Graham became a resident of Penitas.

My mother said that since Judge Gilpin was supposed to be a bachelor, there were certain ladies who set their cap for him, but he escaped in each case, although he was very popular socially. Then, to the surprise of everyone, a daughter came to visit him. I don't know when this was, but the daughter, her Episcopal husband, and her three children came to visit him within my memory — must have been in the early 1880s. We lent them horses to ride while they were here. I think they came from New York.[17]

I don't know just how the judge had his place improved before he went out of the cattle business, but sometime in the early 1870s he sold his entire stock and brand to Uncle Martin and Joseph Wright, of the Motts, a brother of Tom Wright, who had a ranch at Alfred. They paid $30,000 for the cattle and brand, but never used the brand. The Gilpin and Belden brand — the *muneca*, as the Mexicans called it; the American name would have been "cross triangle" — was a simple cross atop a triangle. My uncle Martin told me it was considered the prettiest brand that was in this country in those times. At the time Judge Gilpin sold out for $30,000, that sum of money meant a great deal more than it did later, and certainly many more times that it would today. It must have been then that the Judge improved his place to where it suited me.

However, it had already started to go down when I first remember it. I don't remember that the house was freshly painted; in fact I don't remember what color it was. The windmill was painted red, I think, with alternate spokes of the wheel painted blue and white; the stable was red and had a bronze horse over the door. The paling fence didn't seem to be painted, as I remember, but was outlined with trees, cedar, and some mesquite; there were also mesquites over the yard. A gravel walk, with a fountain in the middle of it, led up to the front steps, under an arbor, and around each side of the house. Grapevines covered the arbor. The water

---

[17] Gilpin was the father of two children, Charles Pope Gilpin, and Caroline Mathilde Gilpin, before he departed for Texas.

from the fountain ran through little ditches lined with plank to different parts of the yard to water the shrubbery and plants. The Judge had lovely roses. At one end of the gallery he had a vine, the queen's wreath, the only one in our part of the country as far as I know. He called it *corona imperial* and said it came from Mexico.

I have gone to Judge Gilpin's when he would be sitting on the broad gallery, with low eaves, smoking his pipe, and Mr. Graham would be sitting there too, smoking his pipe. The Judge was a frail, soft-spoken, blue-eyed, feeble man, with white hair. He spoke in a different accent, although not quite English, however he was of English descent. I wish I knew more of his background. One time Martin Dodson went over to the Judge's on some sort of errand, and it was late in the afternoon. The Judge said to him, "Martin, have you had your tea?" meaning supper, and of course Martin said, "No, Judge, we don't drink tea. We drink coffee."

Through the later years of the life of Judge Gilpin, he went down and down, financially. Finally, Mr. Graham tried to do some farming, cotton, and managed to eke out some sort of a living. After the old cook got too old to do the cooking, and perhaps had little to cook, and nothing to be paid with, he left and moved to San Diego where he had friends. Then Mr. Graham did such cooking as they had. He did all that he could for the old Judge, but he was not fitted to the sort of work he tried to do. It will always be a sad memory to me, especially as I have grown old and realize the pity of the end of the life of a man like Judge Gilpin. Had the scattering neighborhood been more kind and thoughtful, it seems to me this fine old gentleman need not have died in such abject poverty.

One bitter cold night of the winter of 1896-'97, Mr. Graham came for Papa. The Judge had died. Mr. Graham stayed with him until he died, then covered him over, came by the little house where a Mexican was living, sent him to the house, and came on for Papa. When they got back to the Judge, Agapito Sanchez had dressed him and had him laid out. The next day he left for good, and was laid away in the old cemetery in Corpus Christi.[18]

---

[18] He was buried in Old Bayview Cemetery.

Now was the time when the countryside could find time to come. Mr. Reynolds was appointed executor of the estate. The 800 acres of land were mortgaged to Gussett in Corpus Christi, for $1,200. Mr. Reynolds being executor of the estate could not bid on the land, so he had his son John do it. It went for the $1,200 debt. Everything was auctioned off for what it would bring, and of course people not being used to such business would not bid against one another. So what a person bid, they got it for. I believe I know of where only two pieces of the furniture are today. Mrs. Howard Ramey has one of his book cases — there were two filled with books — and Mrs. Maggie McNeill had his desk. Mr. W.G. Sutherland, the schoolteacher, was there and he told me not so many years ago that some books were junked with other things and sold to whomever would buy "the junk." Mr. Si Elliff bid it in. And among the books were four copies of Sir Walter Scott's poems that were first editions — I had read the books, but didn't know their value. Mr. Sutherland said they were priceless, perhaps would have sold for more than enough to pay the ranch out. And the joke was that Mr. Elliff didn't know one letter from another. So, Mr. Sutherland said, when he saw them last they were being thrown around and were about all to pieces. I remember that they were leather-bound. The Judge was a 32nd-degree Mason. All that pertained to the Mason in the way of papers was burned. Mr. Reynolds took some things and I think they finally went to Charley and his daughter Irene has them. I don't know just what they could be, but I have heard her mention that she had them.

So I am sure there are no ghosts at Penitas. I am equally sure there are no buried treasures there. As I understand, the Penitas Ranch took its name from the creek, and the creek took its name from some rocks that are in it some place which I have never seen.

Ruth Dodson (1876–1963) (Plate 25) was born on the Perdido Ranch on Sept. 3, 1876, the daughter of Milton and Susan Dodson. Her early schooling took place on the ranch and, for one year, in the public schools of Corpus Christi. She attended Lagarto College in 1883–84. In 1935, she wrote a volume of Southwest Texas folklore in Spanish, *Don Pedrito Jaramillo* (1934), later published as *The Healer of Los Olmos and Other Mexican Lore*. She also wrote pieces that were published in the *Southwest Review* and *Frontier Times*. Dodson lived at Alice, Texas, and on Catalina Island in California before moving to Mathis. She died at Corpus Christi on July 19, 1963 and was buried in the Old Mathis Cemetery.

CHAPTER 12

J. FRANK DOBIE
RANCH MEMORIES

In writings, big ranches have received most attention, but the little ones have always been more numerous, have aggregated more land, and have raised more cattle, horses and children. Before I enter upon the life of one small ranch, I must approach it as it was approached by my forebears.

My grandfather Robert Neville Dobie (born in Virginia in 1814) and his brother Sterling Neblett Dobie (two years older) were ranching on Middle Bayou in Harris County, Texas, by 1840. One of their neighbors and friends, Francis R. Lubbock, who was to become governor of Texas, left in his "Memoirs" a good account of ranching east of the Brazos River at this time.

In June of 1857 — a panic year — the Dobie brothers contracted to sell all their cattle, but not horses, range delivery, to Sam Allen for $8,500. They probably estimated that they had around 2,500 head of branded stuff. It turned out that Sam Allen was a shrewder estimator. He gathered a lot more cattle than the Dobies thought they had on the open range. In August of this same year Robert Neville Dobie was drowned while bathing in the bayou near his house. Besides his wife, he left three sons; a fourth son was born four months later. That youngest son, Richard (R. J.) was my father.

Early in 1859 Sterling N. Dobie bought a tract of land fronting the Nueces River in Live Oak County and began running *manadas* of horses on the unfenced prairies between the Lagarto and Ramirenia creeks, both of which were living streams, abounding in fish. (A *manada* consisted of about 25 mares with colts, dominated and kept together by a stallion.) Until well into the 1870s many ranches in lower Texas raised more horses than cattle. The Sterling Dobie bands of horses were partly owned by his brother's widow.

In 1875 she moved to Live Oak County with her four sons. All but the oldest (Robert) were ranchers all their lives. The biggest operator among them was Jim (J. M.) Dobie (Plate 31). In 1886, he and my father bought in partnership the ranch I was to be born on. Soon after my father married Ella Byler (lately of Nueces County) in 1887, he bought out Uncle Jim Dobie's half of the ranch.

I was the first of six children and grew up in the Horse Age, wishing for no other life better than one on horseback. Our ranch comprised about 7,000 acres, but Papa, who belonged to open range days and had driven horses up the trail to Kansas, said it was too small to be a real ranch; he had no ambition, as I had, to name it. He was markedly energetic and an active trader. He pastured cattle on the Ed Kilmer ranch in Nueces (now Jim Wells County) and kept land adjoining ours under lease.

A section (640 acres) of the ranch lying on Ramirenia Creek illustrates the history of land as intertwined with the history of people. This section was granted by the State of Texas, through Gov. Wood, to the heirs of August (or Augustine) Brennen in 1848. I have often wished to know who Brennen was and what became of his heirs.

On April 21 — San Jacinto Day — 1866, the tax-assessor and collector of Live Oak County, did, at the courthouse door, offer this section of land for sale to the highest bidder in order to satisfy a claim of 60 cents in taxes due on it for the year 1865. Nobody living now has seen such hard times all over the country as the South had in 1865 and 1866.

Peyton McNeill bid the section of land in for $6, thus covering costs as well as taxes. The Pate McNeill ranch later joined our ranch on the east. I don't know how he was prospering in the intervening years, but on Feb. 3, 1880, the section of land was again sold for delinquent taxes. Four dollars were due on it as taxes for the year 1877, and at public outcry it was knocked down to J. M. Dickens for $9 — $5 to cover costs of the sale. According to law, the owner would have two years in which to redeem the land by paying the $9 plus interest.

Pate McNeill must have redeemed the land, for on April 20, 1880, he sold to W. P. McMaster for $50. McMaster kept it just two months and sold it for $180 to J. M. Dickens, the purchaser at the courthouse earlier in the year. After buying the land, J. M. Dickens built a house on it and lived on it for several years. A cistern beside the house to catch rainwater that he dug into the ground and lined with rock is still visible. Dickens sold the land to Dick and Sterling Dobie Jr., brothers, my father's first cousins, for $1,280 — $2 per acre. Sterling Dobie Jr. sold out his half interest in the land to Dick Dobie, who in 1898 conveyed it to my father for $1,920 — at $3 an acre.

Papa used to recall how Ramirenia Creek was a running stream when he first knew it — before the lands along it were overgrazed, thus making them shed rather than retain the rainfall. When I was a boy the Ramirenia and Lagarto creeks no longer ran constantly but they had good waterholes. Then the waterholes filled with sand and we had to bore wells and put up windmills in the Dickens and Primm pastures, once bountifully supplied with creek water.

One day while Papa and I were waiting in the Primm pasture for another rider, I got down off my horse and looked around on the ground to see what I could see. I picked up a rounded stick, probably oak or ash, sharp at one end with a groove cut in it just below the head. Papa said it was a "stake pin." Some rider had staked his horse on the prairie where I stood, not a bush in sight to tie a horse to. A person would have a hard time now finding in that area a spot of land open enough, free enough of mesquite and other brush, to stake a horse in.

I will not be sentimental and say that the happiest or richest days of my life were spent on the ranch, but I can say as trustworthy Genaro del Bosque, who took care of the ranch after we moved away, used to say: "I have roots here." The longer I live, the more I seem to owe to the land and to my good parents. No play world could have been more interesting than the one I, my older sister and brothers made for ourselves and lived in on the ranch. With pegs, twine and sticks we built big pastures and stocked them with spools, from which my mother's sewing machine had used the thread, for horses; with tips of cattle horns, sawed off in the branding chute in the ranch corrals, for cattle; and with oak galls for sheep and dried small shells for goats. The goats could not be branded, but we branded the other stock with pieces of baling wire heated red-hot.

Trains of empty sardine cans strung together hauled the cattle from ranch to ranch. They were sold for dollars molded in the bottoms of round wooden bluing boxes out of lead melted from empty tin cans and from bullets that had been shot for practice into oak trees. I became a knight in the image of Ivanhoe and with my brother Elrich set up a tournament course, which we ran on horseback, spearing rings.

Tennyson's "Idylls of the King" put me into a world where for months wan lights flickered on plains farther away than Troy. I had heard or read of the music of the spheres, and riding alone one night I thought I heard it; after that I would go out at night to listen to it until I discovered that the sound was made by a variety of katydid. Nevertheless, a certain pulsation of night has continued to seem to come down from the stars rather than go up from the earth.

Our ranch house, the main part of which stands, is in an extensive grove of live oaks on a kind of plateau overlooking the valley of Long Hollow. For most of its distance, this hollow used to be a mere drainage way, its bottom grassed over in places, carrying water only after hard rains, though it could get on a boom then.

Now it is a deep, wide gulch of waste. Erosion. When I first knew it, the valley was a cornfield. Then it was turned out as a part of what we called the Horse Pasture, where the milk cows as well as saddle horses were kept. In time, this old field grew into a dense thicket of mesquites and huisaches. The huisache came to our land not more than 25 years ago. It is beautiful in bloom and beautiful, too, in its grace of green, but it usurps soil without paying anything at all to it or to those who live upon it.

Thousands of times I have looked across Long Hollow valley, and something from those vistas remains deep inside me. In the early morning wild turkeys now and then gobbled from the woods on the far side, and the cheerio call of the bobwhite came from every direction.

On the slope coming down the valley, about half a mile away, stood a hollow, whitened live oak in which buzzards raised their young every year. "Puke like a buzzard" was a common expression of the country, and I used to ride my horse up close to the tree to observe the young white birds, frightened and unable to fly, to verify the saying.

I watched buzzards sail. Nothing in the sky. When I see a buzzard sailing now, the sight takes me back to the sky over our ranch. One spring the bluebonnets on Long Hollow were up to my stirrups. They bloom that high inside me every spring. In my study hangs a little painting of Mexican primroses. It speaks to me of the Mexican primroses I knew as a child.

In spring and early summer I often awake hearing the quick, bright cry made by diving scissortails. They nested in mesquites in the Calf Pasture just north of the house, Long Hollow being to the south. Countless times in these later years a glimpse of the salmon-hued underpart of a flying scissortail has brought back to me those morning awakenings.

The house had a paling fence around it, and in the yard were more flowers — roses, chrysanthemums, cannas, violets especially — than any other ranch in that part of Texas had. The garden, very prolific, was where vegetables grew. The vegetables and the flowers were irrigated from a cypress cistern and a supplementary dirt tank in which a windmill, just back of the kitchen, pumped water. The yard was bare of grass, in the pioneer tradition that guarded against snakes. Occasionally a rattlesnake was killed in it. At the corner of a wide L-shaped gallery to the house — "porch" being a literary word that I never heard spoken — grew a cape jasmine. It happened that at the close of school one year I received a prize of Owen Meredith's "Lucille" with "Il Trovatore" appended.

And I swear as I thought of her in that hour
And how, after all, old things are best
I smelt the smell of that jasmine flower
Which she used to wear in her breast.

When I read those lines in "Il Trovatore," the jasmine by our gallery became affixed to them. Its aroma has never left me.

My mother had some sort of help a good part of the time but often none. With or without help, she was too busy cooking, sewing, raising children and keeping house to garden. Men might come at any hour of the day or night. All had to be fed. My father tended the flowers as well as the vegetables. He set out orange trees, which never bore. He laid out a croquet ground in the shade of oaks. He could do anything from repairing a windmill to making a coffin for a Mexican child that died on the ranch. He was "patron" for some Mexicans who did not live on the ranch. He liked cutting up meat and the meat he butchered was all we had. It was ample. Like many other ranchmen, he never hunted. He hoped his eldest son would choose a career better than ranching — that of a clean-collared banker, perhaps. He paid 8 and 10 percent to his banker and liked him.

Back of the house was a rock smokehouse, long ago crumbled down, for the rock was caliche, not true stone. Every winter my father, aided by Mexicans, killed hogs and cut them up for curing. The only balloons we children knew were the blown-up bladders of hogs and cattle. No child could ask for better. The way to make a bladder expand is to warm it slowly by a fire, gradually blowing air into it through the quill of a turkey feather.

The Mexicans cut long, strong-fibered leaves of bear grass (yucca), heated them lightly over a fire to make them pliable, then used them to tie the hams, shoulders and side bacon to poles across the smokehouse. They were cured by smoke from a fire of corncobs kept smoldering for days on the dirt floor. We had no hickory, needed none. Bear grass will always for me mean homemade hemp, also thatches for Mexican huts.

On back of the smokehouse was a big stable combined with corn crib, hay loft and rooms for tools, saddles and buggies. Along the rear end of it grew a row of pomegranates, so hardy that after 30 years and through the recent drought that killed many oaks, one existed for a while. Their fruit was a treat.

Near them a stout mustang grapevine twined up into the Coon Tree, an oak which a chicken-stealing coon had been seen or shot. High up across the branches, we children had a platform — the "house in the Coon Tree," we called it — which we ascended by the grapevine and on which we often sat reading books or playing and in season (without ice, of course) pomegranateade.

On back of the Coon Tree, adjacent to the barn, were a shed and three pens. The smallest was for the milk calves, which we boys rode; the largest for driving the saddle horses into and for the milk cows. Except in winter, when two or three were fed, there were 12 or 15 cows, all of range breeding, more various in color than productive of milk. Two or three of the mildest-natured cows were willing to adopt dogie calves, and as the dogies were given to us children, we took an especial interest in these foster cows.

The third pen held hay ricks and fronted the horse stalls, but only the buggy horses and work teams were fed. Before daylight somebody — and in time that job was mine — caught the night horse out of the little pasture in front of the house and rode to bring in the remuda from the Horse Pasture. Many a morning I walked stooping over to the ground every few steps trying to skylight a night horse taking his sleep standing up. He always had a drag-rope around his neck, and I would try to get hold of it before waking him.

One dewy morning while I was hunting the saddle horses, the cobwebs were so thick between all the mesquite bushes that I had to keep brushing them away in order to see. They seemed to be raining down out of the foggy sky. The phenomenon came back to me when long afterwards I read Gilbert White's account of a shower of cobwebs in the "The Natural History of Selborne." "Monsieur" Cobweb in "A Midsummer Night's Dream" belonged to the cobwebs in the Horse Pasture, also. Cobweb was our remedy for staunching the flow of blood from a cut or a jab in boy or horse.

The sandy ground in front of the stalls for buggy, hack, tools, harness and saddles had been paved with caliche. Red ants bored through the caliche and colonized below. They are very plentiful in that country and during warm weather work night and day. They have a vicious sting, the pain of which is alleviated by application of wet soda. We saddled our horses on the caliche or close to it.

My father was an early riser, always having coffee boiling long before dawn. When we were running cattle, as the phrase for working cattle went, he had his men away from the house before there was enough light to see by. While we were saddling, the horses would stamp the caliche in order to knock off the red ants crawling above their hoofs.

For several years after I went off to college I half awakened before daylight to the sound of those horses stamping their feet on the caliche. I could hear the low voices of Mexicans saying indistinguishable words, the plopping down of saddles on horse backs, and the metallic clinking of cinch rings and spurs. I never hear those sounds before daylight any more, but the memory of both the actuality and the half-dream is a part of me.

The cattle pens were on down the hill from the ranch house, something less than 200 yards away. The well there was one of the oldest in the country, hand-dug and rock-curbed about 50-feet deep, amid magnificent oaks.

When the wind did not blow during the dog days of August and the big cypress cistern ran empty, water for stock had to be hauled up by pulley. One end of the rope was tied to a large wooden bucket, the other end to the horn of a saddle. Then a boy or a Mexican rode Old Baldy back and forth, back and forth, hour after hour, over a 50-foot stretch, drawing water. I can see my father standing on a wide plank over the well curb and hear his hearty "Whoa!" as the bucket came up and he reached to pour the water into a trough. In time the well was sunk deeper by a driller and cased with iron up even with the old rock curb.

No cattle ever died on our ranch for want of water, but they died on Tol McNeill's ranch west of us, and on the Chapa ranch up about the head of Ramirenia Creek, where my father bought steers. They died on other ranches. I have heard them bawling all night long and all day long for water. No more distressful sound can be made. Men driving herds through the country held them overnight in our pens.

If a thirsty herd came when there was no water, it made too much noise for peaceful sleep.

My mother saw no romance in ranching. The women of her day had no part in riding, scant time to "stand and stare" like cows and watch buzzards sail into infinity. After she moved to Beeville, I heard her express thankfulness that she would never again listen to the bawl of thirsty cattle. Remembering thunder as the voice of hope, I understand how the Hopi Indians worship rain.

It was thirst in summer and hunger in winter for drought-starved cattle. The only reserve of the land is prickly pear. It is composed of about 10 percent fiber and 90 percent water and defends itself by an armor of thorns. Before the portable pear-burner — a flame-thrower fed by gasoline or kerosene and air-pump — enabled one man to singe the thorns off enough pear to feed a hundred cows, men fed a few of the poorest by chopping the pear down, dragging it to a fire in the open, holding it on the end of a green pole over the flames and then pitching it to the slobbering animals.

In January of 1899 Mexicans feeding our poor cows reported that the frozen prickly pear pads were shattering like glass. This was before cottonseed cake became the salvation of poor cattle.

When I was about 10, having learned to read at home long before that, my father and two other ranchers build a schoolhouse on our ranch. Later it was patronized by other families. I must have learned more than I remember from that one-teacher school. We had the best of books at home. I remember some of them vividly, but I will not here go into the deep debts I owe to home reading and the direction of it by my parents, especially my mother.[1]

The jackdaws — grackles, as called now — that nestled in the oaks about our house and lost young ones that we children rescued and made nests for in fence-staple kegs; the calves sucking their mothers and playing about them in pasture; the cows, chewing their cuds in the milk pen; the sandhill cranes fluting their long, long

---

[1] Dobie's mother posted a list of the ten best books for her children to read, which included Pilgrim's Progress, Robinson Crusoe, Ivanhoe, Tom Brown's School Days, A Child's History of England, Plutarch's Lives, David Copperfield, Black Beauty, John Halifax Gentleman, and Heroes and Hero Worship. From Hattie Mae Hinnant New's "Lagarto, A Collection of Remembrances."

cries on a winter evening; the coyotes serenading from every side right after dark; my horse Buck pointing his ears when I walked into the pen to rope out a mount and seeming to ask if I were going to ride him or Brownie; the green on the mesquites in early spring so tender that it emanated into the sky; the mustang grape vines, the fruit too acid to eat raw but superb for preserves and catsup, draping the trees along Ramirenia Creek; the stillness of day and night broken by windmill lifting rods that lifted water; the south wind galloping in the tree tops; the locusts in the mulberry tree and the panting of over-ridden and over-driven horses accentuating the heat of summer; the rhythm of woodcutting in cold weather; the rhythm of a saddle's squeak in the night: these the land gave me. Its natural rhythms and the eternal silence entered into me to remain as long as I remain.

James Frank Dobie (1888–1964) (Plate 30) was born on a Live Oak County ranch, one of six children of Richard and Ella (Byler) Dobie. He lived with his grandparents in Alice a few years until he finished high school, then enrolled in Southwestern University in Georgetown, where he met and married Bertha McKee. He was a reporter for the *San Antonio Express*, where he said he learned how to use the English language. He received a master's from Columbia and joined the University of Texas faculty in 1914. He served in the field artillery in World War I and afterwards resigned from the university to manage his uncle Jim Dobie's ranch. He returned to the university in 1921. His first book, "A Vaquero of the Brush Country," was published in 1929. He published "Coronado's Children" in 1931, "On the Open Range" that same year, "Tales of the Mustang" in 1936, "Apache Gold and Yaqui Silver" in 1939, "Tongues of the Monte" in 1947, "The Voice of the Coyote" in 1949, "The Ben Lilly Legend" in 1950, "The Mustangs" in 1952, "Tales of Old Time Texas" and "Up the Trail From Texas" in 1955, "I'll Tell You a Tale" in 1960 and the "Cow People" in 1964. Dobie wrote about his boyhood life on his father's ranch in Live Oak County for the 75th anniversary edition of the *Corpus Christi Caller-Times,* published on Jan. 18, 1959. Dobie died on Sept. 18, 1964. He is buried in the State Cemetery.

CHAPTER 13

ROY TERRELL
REMINISCENCES

I was born Jan. 2, 1896 on my grandmother Terrell's ranch on the Oso, 12 miles southwest of Corpus Christi. My grandfather — William Blackburn Terrell — who came to Nueces County from Virginia before 1857, died on the second day of December 1889. My grandmother, his widow, Flora Stewart McGregor Terrell, and her three sons — my father, Stewart Blackburn Terrell and my two uncles, William Bayham Terrell and Alfred John Terrell — continued to run the ranch until 1906.

At the time of my birth, Benjamin Harrison was president of the United States. I have lived through 14 administrations and have seen many changes taking place during this time, both nationally and locally.

My earliest playmates on the ranch were Mexican boys — children of ranch hands, and I learned to speak Spanish before English. This cattle ranch, containing 1,600 acres, was sold by the Terrells in 1906 for $9 an acre. It was changed to cotton and truck farming by the new owners and is now dotted with oil wells.

In the period between 1866 and 1872 (before my time, of course) Mexicans raided the country between the Nueces and the Rio Grande and drove off thousands of cattle. All my life I heard about this, and finally, in 1947, the waiting paid off — the Mexican government paid to the descendants of the original ranchers (in this case, my maternal grandfather, Henry Davis Allen) for damages suffered by them. I received some money; in fact, enough was paid to the descendants of my grandfather alone to have bought all the cattle in South Texas in 1866 to 1872. But I didn't argue with them — just took the money. The Terrells never put in a claim for any damage suffered by them.

My maternal grandfather, Henry Davis Allen, came to Nueces County in 1852 from Cherokee County, Texas. His cattle brand was registered, then they turned the cattle loose. There were few fences in those days and the grass and grazing land belonged to any and every one. He never owned any land before his death on May 1, 1874, but his widow, my maternal grandmother, Jane Selman Allen, bought 340 acres on the Oso, adjoining the ranch of my paternal grandparents. She lived there until her death on Aug. 18, 1890. Her children had married and settled on farms adjoining this home place. I was raised with my Allen cousins.

The first school I attended was in a sheepherder's shack on the land originally owned by my grandmother Allen, but which at this time belonged to her son, Henry Davis Allen Jr. The boys would ride their horses to school, stake them out, and the coyotes would chew the ropes in two. When school was out, the horses would have wandered off, but not too far to be recovered. I remember very little about my school days there, but can recall that my twin sister, Ruby, and I would ride to school each morning with the schoolteacher in his buggy.[1]

I only went to this school one year before we moved to Corpus Christi and there I went to the Catholic convent for two years where I learned little except how to pray, an accomplishment I have since forgotten. I then went to the old Central High School on Carancahua Street, which consisted of an eight-room, two-story frame building for the grade schools, and a nearby three-room frame building for high school students. I remember sitting in the

---

[1] That sheepherder's hut on the H. D. Allen ranch was the first school of today's West Oso School District.

classroom and watching them build the new brick high school,[2] which later became Northside Junior High, and which has since been torn down to make way for commercial progress.

The only schools I can remember in Corpus Christi at that time were these two buildings, the school for Mexicans across the arroyo, one for colored students (on the site of the present Coles School) and the Catholic convent. The school was so crowded one semester, when I was in the third grade, that I went to school in a frame building on Water Street; the building was right by the bay.

While I was still a baby, my father built the first road from Corpus Christi to Alice, using convict labor. He was then working as a deputy for the county sheriff. This road followed the Tex-Mex Railroad and was cut out of the brush. If you ever traveled this old road, you would have thought they were all drunk when they laid it off; it was one of the most winding roads ever traveled.

We lived in Alice for a while, when he was working on that end of the road. My twin sister and I were babies and we traveled between Corpus Christi and Alice by train. My mother said she never had to bother with the children on the train; someone was always ready and willing to play with and take care of two babies. My parents had lost three babies before the birth of twins, and so we were rather favored people.

Our transportation was usually by horse and buggy, horses and wagon, or on horseback. My first automobile ride, when I was 12 years old, was in a taxi, the first one in Corpus Christi, which was owned by a man who also ran the livery stable. My father sent this taxi to our house to pick us up and take us to the railroad station, a distance of four blocks, but what an experience! We were catching a train to Calallen,[3] to visit our uncle, Cal Allen, my mother's brother (Plate 33).

---

[2] The new high school, built in 1911 in the 500 block of North Carancahua, was called the Brick Palace.

[3] Calvin J. Allen, a rancher, founded the town of Cal Allen when he convinced the St. Louis, Brownsville & Mexico Railway to bypass Nuecestown and run its line across his pasture. A town called Calvin grew up around the depot, but the name was changed to Calallen.

Traveling by auto was quite a chore — no paved roads, not even the streets in town were paved. The only road that could be traveled in bad weather was a shell road from Corpus Christi to Calallen, following the old stagecoach road, a distance of 15 miles. I made this trip several times with my Uncle Cal, as he had one of the first automobiles in this section. This road was made of oyster shells dredged from Corpus Christi Bay and in spite of all the new four-lane roads adjoining it, it is still known as Shell Road or, by some, as UpRiver Road.

Produce was brought from the ranch over muddy or dusty roads, as the weather permitted. When muddy, six mules would be hitched to the wagon to bring a load of cabbage (one of their chief crops after the ranching business fell off) into Corpus Christi for market and for shipment on the new railroad. It would sometimes take six hours to make the 12-mile trip. There was only one clump of trees and a well, halfway between the two points, and we always stopped there long enough for a cold drink from this well.

I never lived on the ranch after I was eight years of age, but spent a good deal of my time out there visiting my grandmother Terrell, my two Terrell uncles, and my Allen uncles, aunts and cousins.

My grandfather and grandmother Terrell owned two homes — the one on the ranch and one in Corpus Christi. The city house on Mesquite Street, two blocks north of the Courthouse, could have been called their Sunday House, as it was only used when they had to come to town on business or to go to church. In the 1880 census of Nueces County, the William Blackburn Terrell family swelled the population of the United States, as they were listed both on the ranch and in Corpus Christi.

I had another form of locomotion after we moved to town. I was the proud owner of a donkey, which cost $3, and which I rode for several years, finally taking him out to the Allen Ranch and turning him loose in the pasture. My cousin Carl Allen also had a donkey, which he could ride fast enough to use for roping calves.

Before the turn of the century, my grandmother Terrell had a gramophone, which she was always glad to play for her three grandchildren, but we didn't dare touch it. The records were cylindrical in shape and, not to be outdone by the present generation, she had a loudspeaker. One small horn played softly, but the large horn gave out plenty of noise, such as it was. I do not remember any songs on the records — definitely no rock & roll — but they consisted mostly of poems and people talking, about what I do not remember. The only one I do recall was our favorite, "The Raggedy Man," which we asked for more than any other. Bill Lidwell, my cousin on the Terrell side, has this old gramophone now and it is the only family possession, outside of the 1,600-acre ranch, that I would like to have.

The Spanish-American War started when I was two years old. A company of Texas troops was stationed in Corpus Christi, on North Beach; but of course I do not remember anything about this, only what was told me.[4]

In 1904 a railroad was built south from Robstown to Brownsville,[5] and I remember going with my aunt Alice Allen Oliver from her ranch to Robstown in her buggy to deliver eggs to the men who were working on that railroad. I also remember that this Aunt Alice made you eat everything on your plate when you visited her or it was put away for another meal and you ate it then or else. I liked to visit out there in spite of this and the fact that she really made you work when you were around her. My twin sister Ruby wouldn't go to visit out there unless our mother went along to protect her from Aunt Alice's bossing.

On July 4, 1904, there was great excitement — the first train left Corpus Christi for Brownsville over the recently completed tracks and a similar train left Brownsville for Corpus Christi. The train left Corpus Christi at 7:40 in the morning, and got to Brownsville at 7:20 in the evening, almost 12 hours (which later was made by the diesel engines in three hours). Before the building

---

[4] The Longview Rifles, which became Company A of the Third Regiment of Volunteer Infantry, were stationed at Corpus Christi for coastal defense. Some of the men camped on North Beach while others were quartered in the Constantine Hotel.
[5] This was the St. Louis, Brownsville & Mexico Railway, called the Brownie.

of this railroad to Brownsville, the only means of travel south was by stagecoach.

For years, railroading was a big thing. When I came to Kingsville in May 1920 to work for the railroad, there were 600 men employed in Kingsville at the railroad shops. Then trucks, automobiles and airplanes took over their business, just like the railroads took over the stagecoach and freight hauls by horse and wagon in the early days. I have lived to see the day when no passenger train goes through Kingsville.

Due to the development of the Rio Grande Valley and the vegetable and citrus crops, freight trains still pull long strings of refrigerator cars to market in the north and east, using four or more diesel units, with 150 or more freight cars in one train. We could see it coming, but were no more willing to accept it than stagecoach owners were willing to accept the trains when the tracks were first being built across the country.

We didn't go many places when I was growing up. The longest train ride I took as a child was a trip to Armstrong, Texas, about 100 miles south of Corpus Christi, to visit Uncle Mortimer Jefferson Allen (Uncle Mort) on the Kenedy Ranch (La Parra).

Uncle Mortimer met us at Armstrong with a wagon and we went on out to his cattle camp in that. Uncle Mort was *caporal,* in charge of all the cattle on the Kenedy Ranch. He and his Mexican vaqueros lived in tents, but since Uncle Mort was the big boss, his tent had a wooden floor. Although large black spiders ran all around his camp, he wouldn't let anyone kill them.

The cowhands in those days were paid $12 a month and worked from four in the morning until dark. Now the cattle are rounded up with jeeps and airplanes, and a cowboy is seldom seen, except for drugstore cowboys. They wore guns in those days to protect themselves from outlaws and rustlers, but now they only carry rifles to shoot rattlesnakes. This trip was made with Aunt Celia Allen, Uncle Mort's wife, and one of their sons, Carl, just to visit.

I made another trip down there with Carl Allen to visit his dad and two of his brothers, Emmett and Raymond, who were working for the Kenedys. They were farming, raising peanuts to feed the stock. Carl and I spent most of our time hunting geese, ducks and turkeys. There was an abundance of these back then, but we didn't have much luck in our hunting.

Must throw in a story here about Uncle Mort Allen, as told to me by Mike Truan. Mike was working as a boilermaker for the railroad but had worked for Uncle Mort when he was on the Driscoll Ranch, between Corpus Christi and Kingsville.

Uncle Mort was one of the best at breaking wild horses. If there was a horse no one else could ride, Uncle Mort would say, "I'll show you how to ride that horse." They would saddle the horse and Uncle Mort would put a silver dollar in each stirrup under his boots; they would take the bridle off and turn the horse loose; and when the horse stopped pitching, Uncle Mort would still be in the saddle and those silver dollars would still be in the stirrups under his boots.

One of the big events of my life was that on a hot, sultry day, Oct. 22, 1909, President William Howard Taft visited Corpus Christi. My father, Stewart Blackburn Terrell, riding his horse Old Gray, was one of the men who escorted President Taft's car. My father was a member of the Redman Lodge (where they all dressed up like Indians at times) and these Redmen also took part in the ceremonies, but not dressed in Indian garb for this occasion.

My father was a member of the police force and as a mounted policeman is where he shone. John G. Kenedy had given him a beautiful horse and hand-tooled saddle, as my father took care of John when he got on one of his drunks. This horse was traded for Old Gray, described by some as a "flea-bitten gray," but he won many an impromptu race down the main streets of Corpus Christi. In those days, the city policemen spent most of their time roping stray cows and horses off the city streets. Once in a while someone would shoot somebody, but as a rule it was a very peaceful time.

On the momentous occasion of President Taft's visit, I was gathered with all the other schoolchildren of Corpus Christi at the top of the bluff, where we could see the ceremonies and hear the president speak (Plate 32). And we all sang "America" — I imagine it was quite a melodious affair, but we did our best, I am sure — and the president probably recognized it.

In my boyhood, and even in middle manhood, there were few bridges. I remember crossing the Nueces River near the present Calallen on a ferry, where now stands a divided four-lane bridge. I also remember crossing from Corpus Christi north on reefs, which could be navigated by wagons and horses, although the water would come up to the horses' bellies. Now, a concrete causeway spans this stretch of water. Fishing boats were the only boats that could come into Corpus Christi Bay; now, with the deepwater port, ocean-going ships from all over the world dock where we used to fish, swim and hunt.

We had no refrigerators or deep freezers, not even ice; and why we didn't all die of food poisoning is a mystery of the ages. There were very few telephones. The grocery clerk would come from his little grocery store each morning, take the grocery order, and then deliver it to your house. It was a long way from the modern supermarket, but I believe the old way was easier. There wasn't such a selection of food to choose from, and you ate whatever you could find, and it always tasted good. You ordered 25 cents worth of steak, if you had company, and the butcher would throw in enough liver for a meal. No one ever heard of buying liver in those days.

Our water supply was limited. We couldn't turn on a tap and get hot and cold water. Everyone had a wooden cistern to catch rainwater when it rained, and when a long dry spell hit, the cistern would be empty. We had to put potash in this water to kill the wiggletails so we could use it. We bought our water from a Mexican *barrilero* who came by in an old two-wheeled cart with his barrel of water. This was originally gotten from the Nueces River and at that time no one ever heard of purifying the water, so it was not very sanitary, to say the least. Later, it was gotten from the city standpipe, when water had been piped into town from the Nueces River (Plate 34).

Besides buying our water from the Mexican water carrier, we also bought our bread from a Mexican man who came by the door, carrying the loaves of *pan* and *pan dulce* in a large tray on his head. Another peddler was the oyster man — he came around with his buckets of oysters and we bought them by the quart or gallon.

We didn't have too many toys, but Christmas was a time for celebration. We never had a Christmas tree but we always hung our stockings and they were filled with candy, nuts and fruit. There were always a few presents of some kind, and one year my Grandmother Terrell gave me a small wooden wagon. I had seen the Mexican boys at the ranch hitch goats to their wagons and ride around. Living in the city, I didn't have a goat, so I looked around for some other means of transportation. A big strange dog came along about this time and I hitched my wagon to this dog. He took off in all directions, the faster the wagon went, the faster the dog went. When they hit the Tex-Mex railroad track, which wasn't far from our house, my wagon was knocked into many pieces. I gathered up what was left of my wagon but I never saw that dog again.

My Grandmother Terrell was a very indulgent grandmother. She always wore big gathered skirts and in these skirts she had big pockets and in these pockets she always had candy for her three grandchildren.

Someone gave me a calf or two and I became the proud owner of my own cattle brand (Z-3) which is recorded at the courthouse in Corpus Christi. What became of my cattle industry I do not know, but I imagine we ate the calf, or calves, brand and all.

I was large for my age and older than most of the children in my room, as my two years at the convent had put me back scholastically. So while still in grade school I was playing football with the Corpus Christi High School team. In fact, the coach also played on the team. Our equipment was quite different from now. We wore no padding, no helmets, no face or nose guards. The pants and shoes were furnished by the school, but any other equipment — such as shoes with cleats — we had to buy ourselves.

My mother didn't want me to play football, afraid I would get hurt, and how right she was. The first time I went out I sprained my ankle and was laid up for weeks. I played a year after getting into high school. We played Victoria, Beeville, Alice, George West, and Bayview College (located where Portland is now). I don't remember how we got to these towns, but do remember going to George West by train. When we went to Alice to play, they had no high school, and they got together a bunch of college boys, who were home on vacation, and we played against them.

I also played baseball, and one time we went over to Bayview College to play them. We went by train, which ran over a trestle across the bay. We beat Bayview and they told us to get out of town — they were going to run us out if we didn't leave. We told them we had to wait for the train, and they told us we didn't need to wait — so we walked the railroad trestle from Portland to Corpus Christi. We didn't meet a train or I wouldn't be here to tell this tale. One time we went to Petronila to play baseball. We went by horse and omnibus — this was a conveyance with a row of seats running along each side, which we rented from the local livery stable.

School dropouts were not so unusual in those days — very few stayed through high school and fewer still went on to college. I dropped out at the end of my freshman year in high school and went to work. I worked four years at a grain elevator, for 10 hours a day at $1.50 a day. Often we had to work overtime, but there was no such thing as overtime pay.

We worked hard all week, but on Sunday we gathered at someone's house — usually out at the Allens on the Oso — always lots of relatives and visiting neighbors around — and there was always enough for two baseball teams. We had roping contests, tournaments where you ran on horseback with a spear, and we also did all kinds of fancy roping. I had some cousins who were sharks at this. I preferred baseball and can't say that I was ever especially interested in horseback riding, roping steers, and the like.

One of our chief amusements was dancing. Everyone danced. In all modesty, I will have to admit that it was one of my favorite pastimes and I was considered one of the best dancers. These dances started at 8 o'clock in the evening, and we danced until sunrise, with refreshments of cake, coffee and chocolate at midnight. These dances were often held at the schoolhouses. The music was furnished by a Mexican orchestra, usually consisting of three members, one on guitar, one on flute (or some kind of horn) and one on fiddle. The old saying was "Dance up! Daylight's breaking!" Our dances were the square dance, waltz, polka, two-step, schottische, and when we danced we held our partners; none of this across-the-room business. Some people were opposed to what they called "round dancing," where you held your partners in your arms.

About 1906 the Methodist Conference established Camp Epworth along the shore and for 11 years North Beach was used for a summer gathering place for Methodist young people and adults from all over the state. A frame building, called Epworth Inn, was constructed and contained both lodging places and a large auditorium. Smaller buildings went up, and the overflow lived in tents stretched along the sand. Preaching took place night and day, but there was time for games and bathing, as the encampment was right on the bay. There was a big tent where they served meals, at a price of course; and the first time I ever tasted iced tea was at one of these Epworth meetings.

I attended Sunday School at the First Methodist Church (the building was torn down recently) and an annual event was the picnic in the summer. One I remember very well was a trip by train to the Aransas River, about 38 miles from Corpus Christi. We picnicked at the railroad bridge; what we did when we got there I have forgotten. In passing it today by car on the new four-lane highway, our picnic spot looks very desolate and uninviting.

Padre Island, longest of the Gulf islands — 110 miles long, almost as long as Long Island, but much narrower; its greatest width is only four miles — was a desolate, sandy waste, with a few cattle roaming over it, and the only way to reach it in the early days was by boat. Needless to say we didn't go to Padre Island like they do these days. Now, a concrete causeway connects it to the mainland, and Padre Island has been designated a National Park.

Lantern slides were the first form of the present-day movies that we had. Pictures were flashed on a screen and a wild piano player would try to play tunes appropriate to the pictures, but he made mistakes at times and the tune didn't fit the picture. Then we would give catcalls and boos. The first movie I saw was very crude — the only thing I remember about it was that it was a Western and the horses and people moved very jumpily. But we thought it a miracle beyond all understanding that people and animals could be made to move on a screen but the wheels on the vehicles still turn backwards. We advanced from these to better silent movies, then the first sound movies, and now the elaborate screens, with colored pictures and the high-priced movie stars. Can't say that the pictures are much better than our old-time Westerns.

World War I was upon us in 1917 and I enlisted with the Coast Artillery Corps and trained at Fort Crockett, at Galveston, for about a year. We were transferred to the 75th Railroad Artillery and shipped overseas. I was a line sergeant, at $38 a month. They didn't have sergeants like they have now; we just had line sergeant, first sergeant, and mess sergeant. From Galveston we went to Camp Merritt, N. J., for a short time, then down the Hudson River to Hoboken, where we embarked.

We traveled on a boat that had been changed to a transport ship. There were 3,500 soldiers on it and it was so crowded that the bunks were three deep. It was during the flu epidemic and soldiers were dying like flies on the transport. Coffins were piled everywhere. I was seasick the entire nine days of crossing and to this day can't stand steam-cooked food. When we got to France, the flu epidemic was there also and you could see burial details out everywhere burying the dead. Gruesome, but we lived through it.

After we landed at Brest, we did not see action, mostly guard duty. I was at Le Mons when the armistice was signed. Our company was inspected by Gen. John J. Pershing. We sailed for home (welcome words to all of us) in March 1919 from St. Nazaire, France. We came home on a captured German ship that had been made into a transport — not as unpleasant as the trip over to France, but bad enough that I have never had a desire to make another sea voyage. We landed at Newport News, Va., and then traveled by train to Fort Worth, where I was discharged. After having worked for four years at hard labor before enlisting in the army, I enjoyed every minute of my army life, except the seasickness.

Not long after my return from France, on the night of Sept. 13, 1919, I attended a dance at Loyd's Pavilion on a pier on the bay. About midnight we all went home from the dance, and about two o'clock, two hours after we had all gone home, a hurricane and tidal wave struck Corpus Christi. We lived up on the bluff, away from the part of town on the bay, and did not know anything had happened until the morning after. The town was put under martial law and I helped police it. Many people drowned and millions of dollars in damage was done to the part of town under the bluff. My Grandmother Terrell and two of my uncles were living on Mesquite Street, in the second block north of the courthouse, and when the water got into their house, they waded and swam to the courthouse for shelter. My grandmother didn't live very long after this exposure and experience.

After World War I, I worked another year for the same grain elevator until May 1920 when I was offered a job with Missouri Pacific Railroad in Kingsville in order to play baseball with the railroad team. I played six years with this club. During this time I served my apprenticeship as machinist, working on steam locomotives. I worked at my trade until 1954 when all the steam locomotives were discontinued and diesel engines took their place. I had to learn all over on diesels. I continued to do this until Jan. 8, 1960, when I retired, after almost 40 years with the railroad.

It was at one of my first ballgames after coming to Kingsville that I met my future wife. She was an avid baseball fan. I was up at bat and evidently we needed a run or two, and I heard this woman up in the grandstand yelling, "If you ever got a hit, Terrell, get it now!" I asked someone who that was and they told me it was Marguerite McRoberts. During the game a rain came up and we all gathered under the grandstand and she and I started talking. That was in May 1920 and we married on Oct. 1, 1920.

Radio came along, and we had one of the first sets in Kingsville — I still don't know how that sound comes through like it does — but we hovered over our set, with earphones, and would be thrilled because we could get a powerful station out of Cincinnati, Ohio. Instead of telling people about our grandchildren, we spent our time comparing stations that we had been able to bring in.

I saw my first TV in 1948. The screen was about six inches square and only wrestling matches were shown in those days. The groan-and-grunt boys kept us entertained until we found out that the bouts were all fixed, then we lost interest in that sort of program. When we got our first set, Corpus Christi had no TV station and we could only get two from San Antonio. We watched the horrible reception on a snowy screen and thought we were really seeing something. Have seen TV advance into larger and larger screens, and now colored TV; and like the radio, I still don't know how it works. During World War II, I was captain of the Texas State Guard in Kingsville, and trained many boys who went into service. Since I always liked anything military, I enjoyed this part of my war effort very much. I saw my hometown of Corpus Christi grow from a population of not more than 1,500 to the present city of 250,000, and I saw the city limits expand from a small town on the bay to the present city, which takes in most of the county. I saw water, electricity and telephone, inside plumbing, and many other conveniences develop, which were wonderful to us at the time, and which the modern child takes for granted. I believe I have lived through a generation that has seen more development than any other generation, but the future we cannot tell about. Man may be living on the moon before many more years. After 71 years, and all the changes that have taken place in my lifetime, I'm like Judge Crenshaw used to say about the scenery — You drive up to a vantage point, look and say "Oh, my!" I have reached that vantage point.

Roy Terrell Sr. (1896-1980) was born on the Terrell Ranch on the Oso 12 miles from Corpus Christi. His father was Stewart Blackburn Terrell and his grandfather was William Blackburn Terrell. His maternal grandfather was Henry Davis Allen. His mother's brother, Cal Allen, founded the community known as Calallen. Roy Terrell lived on the family ranch, which was being managed by his father and two uncles, William Bayham Terrell and Alfred John Terrell. Terrell attended school in a sheepherder's shack on the Allen Ranch then attended the Catholic school in Corpus Christi and the public schools on Carancahua. He enlisted in World War I and traveled to France by troop transport during the Spanish flu epidemic. After the war, he went to work with Missouri Pacific in Kingsville so he could play baseball for the railroad baseball team. He married Marguerite McRoberts in October 1920. A copy of his reminiscences, as told to Marguerite M. Terrell in April 1967, is in the editor's possession. He died in Kingsville in October 1980.

214

CHAPTER 14

LOUIS RAWALT
ISLAND OF REPRIEVE

I t was the summer of 1925.[1] I was seated near the desk of the chief surgeon in the Military Hospital at Chelsea. The bulky form of the surgeon was across the desk from me. He looked at me with speculative eyes. Finally, he said: "If you have any business that needs attention, you had better return to your home in Texas and take care of it." He leafed through a chart on his desk. "Prognosis: six months." The surgeon looked straight at me. "A lot of them didn't have any time left," he said.

"It'll do," I replied. "It'll have to."

I started for the door. I had expected his verdict, and had already made up my mind what I was going to do — that is, if Viola would consent. I had talked to her about the long white island of the Karankawa Indians, where I had gone as a child with my father on fishing trips. It was the only place I wanted to go . . . a remote, desolate wilderness of sand, whipped by the trade wind, set like a gem between the blue immensity of the Gulf of Mexico and the green shallows of the Laguna Madre on the Texas coast.

---

[1] In another interview with Bill Walraven, Rawalt said this happened in 1927. The latter date is more likely correct. Rawalt said they crossed the Don Patricio Causeway to get to the island and that causeway was not built until 1927.

I had met Viola through her brother, who was also a patient in the Chelsea Hospital. We were married in a few months. Viola was young, vital, beautiful, and accustomed to the cultured atmosphere of Boston. Would she catch the vision of Padre? Would she go there with me to spend the few months that the military doctor had given me to live? That night, I spun my dream to her, a dream of the primitive island, untamed and uninhabited. Her eyes sparkled as I talked. She kicked off her shoes and did a little war dance, "Padre, here we come!"

For the first time since that soul-shattering verdict of death, I faced the future with a degree of hope. From that moment my mind was turned from its dark remembrance of World War I, with its aftermath of destruction. The doctors had done their best. In one hospital I had relinquished a kidney, in another a part of a lung. Along the way I had lost my vitality and more than 50 of the pounds that normally covered my six-foot frame.

So, travesty of a bridegroom that I was, I sat beside my wife and together we laid the groundwork for a strange future. I could see that this healthy young wife of mine could not comprehend the fact that it was only to be an interlude, and I was thankful for her optimism.

We took a train for Texas the next day. In Kingsville, we spent a few days with my people while assembling the equipment essential for living on an isolated island. The upper end of Padre is only 25 miles from Corpus Christi; yet then it was considered inaccessible to all but a few intrepid souls who would risk their cars and their necks crossing the crude wooden causeway[2] that snaked its way across the treacherous waters of the Laguna Madre. My father had been one of those who dared. Together we spent many days on the island before my martial peregrinations. While he sat on a box or a log, fishing with his cane pole at the edge of the great

---

[2] Col. Sam Robertson built the Don Patricio Causeway connecting the Flour Bluff road from Corpus Christi with the island. The three-mile causeway was built over the water with wooden troughs for car wheels. This two-way causeway of military design was built in 1927 and lasted until it was destroyed by a storm in 1933.

rolling waters of the Gulf, I tramped the beach and prowled the dunes.

Many times Pop laid his pole down, back out of reach of the tide, and came looking for me thinking that I was lost. I was lost, but only in the newness of this ageless island. At times the beach, between the water and the dunes, was as clean as a whistle. It looked as though it had been washed and smoothed by a giant trowel with only huge driftwood logs jutting up here and there to break the monotony. Again it was covered with litter from the seas — Seaweed, shells, jellyfish, and the flotsam and jetsam from ships. Nothing was too small or insignificant for close observation.

Back of the sentinel-like row of dunes, I found the happiest hunting ground of all when I came one day upon a flat where the wind had swept away the sand to reveal countless spear points and arrow heads. Then I was back in a lost century where breech-clouted Karankawas fought invading Comanches with their backs against the blue wall of the Gulf.

I wandered through coarse grass and over miles of blown sand, powdery and white. I stopped to pick up bits of pottery and to examine strange, unnamable growths of vegetation. Curlews flew high over the swaying tops of the sea grasses crying shrill warnings to their mates. Sandhill cranes waded the inland ponds and great blue herons clustered on the dunes. Occasionally, I saw the tawny form of a coyote watching me suspiciously from a distance. Jackrabbits leaped from clumps of grass, and I saw the dens of badgers and ground squirrels. I used to wish that I could explore every inch of the 132 miles of the islands, for Padre and Mustang were often joined together when the pass between them filled up with sand. Padre itself is 110 miles in length and varies in width from two to seven miles.

This was the island to which I was taking my wife, and where I meant to spend my rapidly dwindling lifetime. Certainly, Padre was not an island of story-book enchantment. Rather, it was a place of realities so stark and primitive that they gave an impression of unreality. The suns of long summers beat down on it with merciless intensity increased by reflection of sand and sea. Hurricanes periodically lashed its shores; huge driftwood logs and the hulks of

217

boats rotting in the sand far above normal tide line bore evidence of their force. In winter the blue Texas northers roared down across the plains and sent the sand swirling and drifting like snow in a blizzard.

Once in Kingsville, we lost no time in assembling our equipment. I bought a Model-T Ford for a nominal sum of money. Into the back of it went a small tent, two army cots, a gasoline camp stove and a lantern. We took plenty of blankets and the necessary clothing and cooking utensils. When I say necessary, I mean that — tin plates and cups, a skillet, a stew kettle, and some knives and forks. We took a month's supply of food, mostly staples and canned stuff. We took a saw, hammer and nails. Viola stored her lovely china and linen, a little grudgingly, but she glowed with a spirit of adventure that was good to see.

We left Kingsville on a sunny September morning. Behind me were the years of war, the hospital corridors, the waiting rooms, and the operating tables. I kept the doctor's grim predictions from my mind as much as possible.

Keeping the wheels of the Model-T on the parallel planks of the causeway demanded all my attention, but every few moments Viola would cry out over some strange bird flying over Laguna Madre. There were white pelicans by the thousands, snowy egrets, roseate spoonbills, herons, ducks, gulls and terns. Mullet leaped and played in the water, shining like new silver in the bright morning sun.

We left the causeway and followed a winding path through the dunes to the Gulf side of Padre. At the beach, we turned left, and drove along the surf to Corpus Christi Pass where we set up camp. The pass was open then, and the islands of Padre and Mustang were divided. I don't know what time we reached the pass; we took no clock with us. I didn't want time measured out to me in minutes and hours.

We gathered lumber the rest of that day to build a floor for the tent. Viola did most of the labor, for there was little strength left in my body. When the sun was high, we stopped long enough to eat the lunch Mother had packed for us. It had been many months since food had tasted so good, and if the fried chicken was seasoned with a little Padre Island sand, we neither noticed or cared.

By nightfall we were snug and secure. We ate a supper of bacon and pork and beans by the light of our Coleman lantern. Viola had made a table from a small hatch cover the tide had carried in; our chairs were two nail kegs. She stacked some apple boxes, one above the other to make a cupboard for our supplies. The cots were set up, side by side, at one end of the tent. We turned out the lantern, brushed some sand from our bare feet and crawled between the covers.

"I love that lantern," Viola said sleepily. "It gives you time to get in bed before it goes out." I listened to the pounding of the surf a moment before sleep overtook me. From the dunes behind us coyotes howled.

I woke that first morning feeling refreshed and eager to face the day. I raised the flap of the tent to see the splendor of early morning on the Gulf. Nature was outdoing herself in artistry. The sky, the water, and the clouds along the horizon were all tinted with color — mauve, rose and copper seeping through the gray. As I watched the sun break through to make a golden path across the water, Viola came softly on bare feet to stand beside me. I had everything. But for a limited time only.

That day and the ones following it flowed by. The hours came and went like the waves that broke against the sand, unmeasured and unrecorded. We ate when we were hungry. When we were tired, we rested. When the time came for sleep, we slept like exhausted children. For the most part, Viola busied herself around the camp. But sometimes she came and dropped down beside the camp chair where I sat for hours at a time fishing with my cane pole.

Gradually, the sun and the salt air worked their healing magic. Before many weeks had passed, I felt the beginning of strength returning to my body. The aches and pains lessened. The shadow of death lingered, but grew fainter.

Our appetites were enormous. In spite of all the fish we ate, our supplies disappeared rapidly. Neither of us looked forward to the trip to town after more. Fish were plentiful in those days and would strike at anything, even a bare hook. I saw schools of redfish a mile long, their color like a river flowing through the Gulf. There were many other species of fish, and I think I caught some of them all. There were redfish, trout, drum, pompano, pike, mackerel, golden croaker, whiting, and many less important fishes. The bottom of the lagoon was thick with flounder which we gigged at night by lantern light.

One cool night in October I caught 500 pounds of redfish on my trot lines. Early morning found us chugging across the causeway with our load. The fish sold for $25. Then we bought supplies and more line and hooks and hurried back to our island as fast as the Ford would take us. After that, I fished commercially.

When the first norther whistled down across the dunes, we realized that we would have to have a stove to keep the tent warm. So the next trip to town we bought some stove pipe, a chisel and some hinges. I took an oil drum and chiseled out a door on one side and hinged it on. For the pipe, I cut criss-crosses and flanged them out to fit tight. We filled the drum about a fourth of the way up with sand for insulation on the bottom, ran the pipe up through a hole in the tent, and there was our stove. Wood was no problem. The tide took care of that, but cutting it became my chore. Viola tried it once, but swore off tearfully after a stick of wood flew up and hit her in the eye.

Winter passed. A short spring merged into a long summer. By next October, I realized that I had borrowed six months over my allotted time to live, and by leave of the Almighty I meant to borrow as many more as I could. I was strong again and seldom felt the touch of pain. Fishing was good, and if the proceeds in those days were not astounding, there was always enough for the things we really needed. Island living agreed with Viola. She was brown and healthy and as active as a ground squirrel.

We moved our camp to the edge of Big Shell the next year, 35 miles down the beach. This time we had a shack to live in — a place loaned to us by Major Swan, one of the old-timers on the island. I bought a surf net and a used Model-A to replace the rust-eaten Model-T. We converted the Ford into a pickup. Viola helped me with the net until I found a fishing partner.

One morning when we were hauling in the net something kept leaping against it with the force of a huge shark or a porpoise. We couldn't bring it in, so I staked one end of the net into the sand, and hooked onto the other end with the car. Slowly I pulled in the net until the creature lay in the edge of the surf. Incredible! It was an 18-foot sawfish. When some fishermen came by later that day and found me beside the sawfish with a cane pole — no net in sight — they assumed I had caught it with the pole. I didn't enlighten them and this tall fish story was told about Corpus Christi for years. The sawfish, I regret to say, became food for the packs of coyotes that roamed the wild stretches of Big Shell.

We seldom saw other human beings there, but coyotes prowled close to our shack at night, and in the early mornings and evenings we saw them on the beach searching for fish, the mainstay of their diet. I learned by experience just how clever and crafty they were. I have seen them fishing in the surf for mullet and catching them! Many times I saw these lean hungry animals watching me from over the rim of the dunes. Once I left the beach, they would sneak down and pick up my discards. Sitting on the porch that I had added to our shack, one early morning after I had set out my trot-lines, I saw two big coyotes slink down to the water's edge and begin dragging one of the lines to shore. I was too amazed and curious to move. They pulled the line all the way in, then bit the fish off the hooks, and trotted with them back to their habitat in the dunes. Many persons doubted the truth of this, but I saw the same thing happen time and again.

One night Viola nudged me awake. "There's something in the kitchen," she whispered. Listening, I heard the faint rattle of the tin plates we left on the table. I got up and edged toward the kitchen. The moonlight streamed through the open door and outlined the gaunt gray form of a coyote. He was on the table licking up the remains of our supper. He sensed my presence and leaped for the door, but slipped on a greasy plate and somersaulted into the center of the room. I gave a swift kick to the astonished animal and sent it rolling down the back steps. Tail down, it trotted up a dune and sat on its haunches barking with anger. As I looked closer, I saw the forms of four or five puppies, joining in the harsh chorus. They continued to bark until I got my shotgun, then they vanished into the night.

During a big run of redfish I caught 90, averaging in weight from five to 15 pounds. I kept them on stringers alive in the surf until I was too tired to fish anymore, then, nearing midnight, I started to ice them down in the pickup. There was no ice. I hastily loaded the fish and hauled them back of the dunes where I put them in a pond. We could net them the next morning easily and rush them to market. This catch would bring $70 or $80, which we needed for supplies.

Satisfied with the night's work, I tumbled into bed and slept until dawn. With the first light of morning, I hurried to the pond. I stared in amazement at what I saw. Scattered around the banks of the pond were the headless carcasses of the 90 redfish. The coyotes had outwitted me. Their tracks formed a network around the pond and trailed into the sand dunes in every direction. They ate a hearty supper, but what were we going to eat?

I drove into town that day for a new supply of ice, which was all I could buy. The next night the redfish were still running — so we got our groceries and gasoline after all.

Coyotes weren't the only problem we had to cope with on the beach. In any season, but especially during the vernal and autumnal equinoxes, the Gulf might change from peace to violence. We lived in the Devil's Elbow, the bend of the long arm of Padre. It was strewn with the accumulated wreckage of the years, from shrimp boats and freighters to Spanish galleons dating back to the time of Cortés. Salvage from these boats helped us improve our daily living conditions. Some old coins and jewelry I found at the site of one of the wrecks made interesting additions to our treasure trove of beach-combings.

Some of the castoffs of the waves were unusual and astonishing. One afternoon Viola and I stopped to examine a five-gallon can that had washed up on the beach. I pried the lid off with my fishing knife. The can was filled with clean white lard. We put it in the pickup and before the day was over we had salvaged more than 100 cans. There were more damaged cans that we left lying on the beach. The Coast Guard told us later that a Mexican freighter had been torn to pieces by a sudden tumult in the Gulf. She was carrying a cargo of lard. It was a profitable load of salvage for us and a grease bath for the beach. For a long time after that the sand was saturated with lard. The island coyotes grew fat from feasting on it. Even the sand crabs acquired a new look of sleekness.

It was about the same time when the British smuggling vessel named *I'm Alone* was shelled and sunk by a Coast Guard cutter in Sigsbee's Deep near the southern tip of Padre. The ship was spotted off New Orleans where she expected to land her contraband cargo of whisky. The cutter chased her along the coast, finally closing in on her. The captain refused to surrender. He jettisoned the cargo before the Coast Guard cutter blasted the ship full of holes.

I received word through the island grapevine to be on the lookout for liquor, so I started down the beach in the pickup, searching the incoming waves and the tide-line for bottles of the amber elixir. I didn't see anything that looked like whisky, but noticed a full gunnysack imbedded in the sand. I could check it later, so I drove on, but when I saw several more similar sacks, I stopped to investigate. The sack I opened contained a dozen sealed tin cans. I pried the lid from one of the cans. Inside was a bottle of "Old Hospitality" bourbon whisky.

During the day, I salvaged 110 sacks. I stashed this horde behind the dunes, filled a duffle bag with 72 bottles, and headed for Port Isabel. The ferry boat took me across the channel. The captain's suspicions were aroused by the weight of the duffle bag. I had to explain what I had found and make a gift of a few bottles. It is enough to say that I disposed of the remainder in the duffle bag in Port Isabel.

When I returned to the island, a comforting feeling of cash in my pockets and the prospect of more, I met the captain of the ferry boat and one of his crew. They were driving a pickup with the bed loaded with familiar looking gunnysacks. I followed their tracks, as they had, from all appearances, followed mine, to my cache in the dunes. Of all my loot, there wasn't even a bottle left.

For weeks thirsty men combed the beach all the way from Port Isabel to Port Aransas. At Port Aransas, one boatman got more of the drink than he counted on. He spotted a sack and headed his craft toward it. As he reached over the side for the bobbing burlap bag, he fell into the water. He was five miles from shore and his boat was circling away. He kept afloat by using the liquor as a lifebuoy. The boat swung in a circle, finally closing back to him. He grasped the side and struggled aboard. Evidently, the thoughts that raced through his head as he floundered in the water, with drowning almost a certainty, sobered him greatly. When he got back to town, he sold his boat and other possessions and moved inland.

The days flowed into weeks and the weeks became months and years. I had grown steadily stronger and seldom gave a thought to the fact that I wasn't supposed to be alive. I could walk for miles without tiring. Many nights I slept on the sand with only a piece of tarpaulin around me when I was fishing away from camp. It was one of the times when I had gone alone to a spot 35 miles below our shack that the car stalled. No amount of coaxing or tinkering could get a sound out of it. There was nothing to do but start walking. It was 70 miles to Corpus Christi Pass where someone lived who had a car. The tide was exceptionally high, and I had little hope that any fishermen would be venturing down the beach that day.

It was early morning when I started out. A little before sunset I reached our shack. Viola was visiting my people in Kingsville at the time. The place was still and had an empty feeling. I ate, drank some coffee, and rested for a few moments before starting again. The tide was rising rapidly. It looked as though a storm might be brewing in the Gulf. If I didn't get the car up out of the reach of the water, I wouldn't have a car.

This thought kept my bare feet plodding through the sand all night. It was dark as pitch. Sudden squalls blew in, keeping me drenched most of the time. But with the first gray light of morning, I could see by the familiar outlines of the dunes that I was only a few miles from the pass.

Bill White, another fisherman, was cooking breakfast in his tarpaper shack when I knocked at his door. I was too tired to eat, but as I gulped down scalding cups of coffee, I couldn't help crowing over the fact that four years before I had been doomed, given six months to live. Yet in the past 24 hours I had walked 75 miles!

During the next year I acquired a fishing partner. We called him Shorty and if he had any other name we never knew it. He was a good man on the end of a net. It relieved Viola from some pretty hard work. She had found a bale of cotton washed up on the beach and subsequently launched a quilting project. Shorty set up his tent a little beyond our shack and until the hurricane of that year,[3] we had a pleasant and profitable partnership.

That was the year the Gulf staged a real shindig. We had several scares that September. Viola kept most of our valued and important possessions packed in boxes against the time we might have to evacuate. The Friday before the storm hit on Monday was one of the most perfect of island days. The water was flat and blue. The skies were clear and the southwest wind was warm and gentle. Shorty was expecting weekend guests and Viola, thinking they would perhaps visit us too, had unpacked the boxes and made the house cozy and neat.

I was fishing early Saturday morning when I noticed that the swells were coming over the beach in an erratic rhythm. Far out over the water the sky had an ominous look. Wildlife deserted the beach. A squall hit with sudden intensity. I pulled in my line and went into the shack. Viola was still sleeping. I woke her and told her to get ready to go to town, that I thought there was a storm on the way. Sleepily, she started pulling on her jeans and shirt, mumbling about repacking everything. I walked to the porch and looked out. The tide had risen so fast that it was already hazardous to travel the beach.

"You won't have time for that," I told her. "We'll have to go now or not at all."

Shorty came in. He had seen the signs. There was no need to tell him. Another squall hit as we were getting into the pickup where we were squeezed in together. The beach was almost impassable where the long sweeps crowded us up into the soft sand and shell. But the Model-A came through and in late afternoon we reached the house of friends in Corpus Christi.

I checked with the Weather Bureau and found that there was, indeed, a storm in the Gulf. It was one of exceptional force and was

---

[3] He was referring to the storm of 1933, which destroyed the Don Patricio Causeway.

headed straight for the Texas coast. They expected the storm to hit on Monday. After getting Viola more or less safely settled, Shorty and I began to talk about returning to the island and going down the beach at low tide that night to save some of our equipment. We decided to go and, over Viola's protests, we refueled the Ford and drove back over the causeway to Padre.

The island was a place of darkness and fury that night. It rained incessantly and the wind blew in gusts that threatened to topple the pickup. We had only gone a mile or two down the beach when we both had to admit that it was hopeless to try to go farther until daylight. So we drove the Ford up into the edge of the dunes and sat there all night trying to sleep, our legs cramping and the water reaching nearer with every heave of the Gulf.

When morning came, the rain let up a little. We shoved and shoveled our way through the dunes and to the grasslands in the center of the island. It took all day to reach the shack, driving over rough terrain and through the pools of water left by the night's deluge. It still rained and the wind blew.

We left the truck behind the dunes and walked over to the house. The water was running under it so deep it was over our knees as we waded up to the steps. We estimated that the tide was four or five feet above normal. I knew that unless some miracle happened, the shack was not going to stand much longer. I went inside and dumping a pillow out of its case started grabbing some of the valuables and putting them into the pillowcase. I tossed in a box containing several old coins I had found among the wreckage of an old ship, a rust-encrusted pendant I had picked up at the site of the Padre Balli mission ranch. Then there were the stem-wind gold watches I had found in a wooden box on the beach and my collection of arrowheads and spear points.

I was looking around at all the rest of our furnishings and equipment, wondering how much to take, when a giant roller hit the shack with terrifying force. I felt the floor sway and buckle under my feet. The water was running up through the cracks when I went out the back door with a pillow case in one hand. The steps had washed away. As I jumped off the porch into the water that was now over waist-deep, I caught sight of a can of gasoline that I was counting on to use for the return trip to town. I caught the can as it floated by me and waded out of the maelstrom. Shorty, having collected his belongings from the tent, was waiting for me in the truck.

I put the gasoline in and looked back at the house. It had toppled over and was being beaten to pieces by the waves. When I started to place the pillowcase on the seat, I discovered I had grabbed the wrong one. I had salvaged only a pillow and a can of gasoline which might not even be enough to get us back to town. Darkness was coming on fast. The storm grew in intensity. We would be lucky if we got out of it with our lives.

Fortune was kind to us that night. By following our recently made tracks back up the center of the island, we carefully made our way to the north end of Padre. There we found the waters of the Laguna Madre lapping over the plank troughs of the causeway. Could we make it? The choice had to be made quickly. We would try. So I nosed the Model-A onto the planks and we inched our way over the water. Wind tore at us and the rain poured down in torrents.

It was daylight by then — a liquid gray daylight in which everything blended and wavered like the scenes in an underwater film. At the ship channel we found that the swing bridge had been torn partly loose. The ends of it were two feet higher than the planks of the causeway. A barge was anchored nearby with several men aboard. They came to our rescue. Climbing from the barge to the causeway, they lifted the Ford and set it on the bridge. Then they set it down at the other end. Thus we finally reached the comparative safety of the mainland.

Later we learned that during the next hour after we had crossed the causeway was reduced to a total wreck. The planks were torn loose and flung into the air. Some of them were found weeks later in the mesquite forests of the King Ranch, 20 miles away.

That hurricane left devastation everywhere it moved. Much of Corpus Christi was a shambles. Padre Island was cleared of everything for a hundred miles. The contours of the beach were changed and there were 30 channels cut all the way from the Gulf to the Laguna Madre.

Within a week after the storm, we were back on the island. We got there by loading our car on an improvised raft and poling it across the Laguna Madre. Driving the beach was hazardous. It was stripped with deep ruts and covered with logs and debris. The passes were filling up with sand, and we were able to drive through them, although we drove through water two feet deep in places.

At the site of our former shack there was nothing. Nothing, that is, except an old ice-box half sunk in the sand. Shorty's tent had caught around the ice-box and on examination showed its only damage to be a small rent. In searching about the campsite, he found all the things he had left with the exception of a small stew kettle. As I said, Viola and I found nothing. Out of all the supplies — the equipment, the bedding, the clothing — not a sign of anything. Yet Shorty found everything he owned except for a 35-cent kettle!

The ways of the sea are strange. They say that whatever it takes away from you it brings back. I'm inclined to think that it does. The next few months the tide carried in the lumber and piling for us to build a bigger and stronger house. This time we built 65 miles from the north end of Padre.

The following years, my time was divided between fishing and exploring the lower end of the island. When we were in town, I went to the libraries and lost myself in the fascinating history of Padre. The lore of Indians, pirates, and of the early settlers who had tried unsuccessfully to conquer the sands, had long held great interest for me. But the knowledge of Padre is accumulative. Before long I was delving into geology and ornithology.

Viola spent much of these last few years in town. About 20 years ago, we discovered a new species of bird circling above our shack. It was a stork. Since it seemed reluctant to leave its bundle on the wild stretches of Padre, we started paying on a home in Corpus Christi. The bundle came and we called her Louise. Later the stork paid us another visit; this time it was a boy whom we called Charles.

The four of us spend many rich and contented hours of summers and vacations on the island, but the children had to go to school so we have maintained our home in town. Viola is happy being a mother and housekeeper during the seasons when she has to stay at home. But when summers come we spend the time together on the beach. My work keeps me on the island much of the time, but even when there is no necessity, the pull of the blue distances overcomes me. Now, 30 years after the doctors predicted my imminent death, I roam the wilds of my island like an aging Karankawa Indian.

Louis Enoch Rawalt (1899-1980) fought in four major battles in World War I and after the last one was listed as missing in action. He was found wounded, the victim of a gas attack, after the Armistice. In the army of occupation, he attended the Sorbonne in Paris. He returned to the home of his parents in Kingsville, then re-enlisted in the Army. He attended the University of Texas, then joined the Navy. In 1925 he was discharged from the Navy with a kidney infection resulting from his old shrapnel and poison gas wounds. The Navy doctor told him he had only a few months to live. He married Viola Mae Bell, whose brother was a patient in the same military hospital. They moved to Texas and lived in a tent and then a shack on the beach on Padre Island. Rawalt spent his days fishing and beachcombing and regaining his strength. They had two children, Charles Rawalt and Louise Rawalt (later Mrs. Louise Williamson). Rawalt's sister, Marguerite Rawalt, was a pioneer leader of women's rights and one of the founders of the National Organization of Women. Rawalt died on Jan. 29, 1980 — 55 years after doctors told him he had six months to live.

INDEX

Baurop, Charles: 43, 44
Baxter, Peter: 35
Bayside, Texas: 45
Bayview Cemetery (Old): 12, 35, 76, 94, 98
Bayview College: 209, 210
Beaman, Charles: 87
Bee, Bernard E.: 21, 65
Bee, Gen. Hamilton P.: 21, 22, 65, 72
Beeville: 71, 211
Belden, Frederick: 3, 4, 11, 32, 65, 84, 93, 94, 180, 181, 182, 187
Belden, Mauricia (née Arocha): 93, 94
Belden Ranch (Carmel): 181
Belden, Sarah: 65
Bell, Viola Mae (Rawalt): 215-229
Belle Italia, ship: 30, 33
Benavides: 140
Benson, Pete: 44
Berry, Doc: 91
Berry, Henry W.: 26, 27, 59
Beynon, Tom: 139
Bidwell Hotel: 85
Biggio, William: 44
Big Shell: 220
Blucher, C. F. H.: 39, 89, 94
Blucher, Dick: 89
Blucher, Felix von: 20, 21, 35, 76, 94, 97
Blucher, George: 47, 89, 94
Blucher, Julia: 67
Blucher, Marie von: v, vii, 15, 23, 25, 83, 98, 160, 177
Blucher, Mary Felicia (Downing): 35, 149
Blumenthal, M.: 85
Borden's Ferry: 36, 40
Borden, Gail: 37
Borden, Sidney: 36, 39, 42, 144, 145, 167, 174
Borjas Ranch: 139-146, 153
Bragg, Braxton: 63
Brazos River: 191

Breakers Hotel: 26, 88, 139
Breakers, ship: 39, 95
Brennan, Ed: 46
Brennan, Mike: 46, 161
Brennen, August (or Augustine): 192
Britton, Anne Elizabeth (Davis): 60, 62, 63, 65
Britton, Edward: 60
Britton, Forbes: 6, 18, 19, 27, 57, 59, 60, 61, 66, 81, 82, 88, 113
Britton, Malvina (Moore): 57, 67, 82, 110, 113
Britton Motts (Britton Ranch): 19, 60, 81, 148, 175
Britton, Rebecca (Worthington): 60, 61
Brooks, W. H.: 9
Brown, Gen.: 98
Brown, Lt. John S.: 94
Brown, W.B.: 94
Brownsville: 10, 21, 22, 23, 31, 35, 62, 90, 93, 96, 98, 146, 205
Brundrett, George: 180
Bryden, James: 7, 174
Bryden, Mary (Barnard): 148
Buckley, Ed: 41, 138, 173, 174
Buckley, Mrs. Ed: 173, 174, 177
Bulk Head: 37
Burks, Dr.: 50
Burriss, Bass: 147
Büsse, Frederick: 67

Cahill, Cornelius: 66, 71
Cahill house: 27
Cahill, Tom: 85
Calallen: 36, 133, 134, 171, 203, 204, 208
Calcasieu, La.: 42
Caldwell, Edward Harvey: viii, 47, 988 117, 137-153
Caldwell, E. L.: 25, 55
Caldwell, George: 139, 142
Caldwell's Hardware: 118
Caldwell, Lafayette: 174

Gravis, John A. F.: 3, 26, 27, 59
Gravis, Mrs.: 3
Gray, Mustang: 17
Green Lake: 46
Gregory, William S.: 23, 68
Guadalupe River: 11
Gussett, Horatio: 9, 49, 150
Gussett, Leona (Givens): 9, 175
Gussett, Susie: 9
Gussett, Norwick: 9, 41, 87, 88, 138, 139, 148, 149, 175, 184
Gussett, Norwick Jr.: 9
Gussett, Susie: 9
Gussett Wharf and Warehouse: 88, 139
Gussettville (formerly Fox Nation): 9, 186, 187
Guth Park (downtown): 71

Halifax, Nova Scota: 179
Hampton, Mr. and Mrs. Wade: 149
Hannah, sloop: 29, 95
Harbor Island: 28
Hardin, Jack: 29, 95
Harney, Gen. William S.: 66, 71
Hart, Elizabeth: 2, 5
Hatch, George C.: 5,
Hayes, Mary Eliza (Dix): 65, 78, 82
Headen & Son: 40
Headen, Bessie: 158
Headen, William: 64, 90, 158
Healy, Margaret Mary (see Mrs. J. B. Murphy)
Hearn's Ferry: 40
Heath, Capt. Cheston C.: 41
Helena, Texas: 6
Henrietta, mailboat: 46
Henry, Julius: 138
Heritage Park: 95
Hidalgo Seminary: 86, 87, 95
Hill, E. P.: 89
Hinnant, Mary Ann: 15
Hinojosa, Pedro: 59
Hirsch, David: 138

Hobbs, George: 147
Hobby, Maj. Alfred Marmaduke: 155
Hoffman, Prokop: 7, 177
Holbein house: 85
Holbein, John: 17
Holbein, Reuben: 17
Holden, Mrs. Green: 46
Hollub Courthouse: 121, 151, 163
Hollub, Maj. Rudolph: 106, 121, 151
Holterhaus, Jim: 91
Holthaus, Mr. and Mrs: 5, 9, 11
Holy Cross Cemetery: 60
Hooper, Frank: 49
Hopson, C. R.: 2
Horton, Rev. H. J.: 146, 147
Houston: 180
Howard, Dean S.: 4,
Howell, Joe: 167
Hubbard, Capt.: 37
Hubbard, Mary B. (Kinney): 66
Huck & Halfrench: 46
Hunsaker building: 85

I'm Alone, ship: 223
Indianola: 6, 17, 35, 39, 45, 46, 69, 139
Inez Houston, lumber schooner: 43
Ingleside: 5
Ireland, John: 35
James, J. T.: 152
Japonica, ship: 55, 105
Jim Wells County: 14, 15, 23, 101, 103, 128, 192
Johns, Glover: 68
Johnson, Dan: 52
Johnson (probably Johnston), Dr. G. F.: 76, 77
Jones Building: 69
Jones, Dr. Levi: 81, 149
Jordt-Allen: 149

Kearney, Dr. Thomas: 44, 67, 76, 77, 152
Keller, Mrs. Amanda: 26

ACKNOWLEDGEMENTS

Many thanks are offered to those who supplied the photographs used in Recollections: Bruce and Ellenita Collins (Plate 1), Jane Adams (Plate 3), Corpus Christi Public Library, Grace Charles of the Special Collections and Archives, Texas A&M University. Most of the images come from the collections of Murphy Givens and Jim Moloney. We would also like to thank Allison Ehrlich of the Corpus Christi Caller-Times for permission to reprint J. Frank Dobie's account of his early years on his father's ranch in Live Oak County. It was first printed in the 75th anniversary edition of the Caller-Times on Jan. 18, 1959.

BOOKS FROM NUECES PRESS

RECOLLECTIONS Of Other Days

GREAT TALES From the History of South Texas

A Soldier's Life

Corpus Christi – A History

1919 – The Storm – A Narrative and Photographic History

www.nuecespress.com

www.ingramcontent.com/pod-product-compliance
Lightning Source LLC
Chambersburg PA
CBHW020338100426

42812CB00029B/3170/J